Introuauction

Kathryn Galloway was born on March 30, 1965, in Selma, Alabama, to Rev. George Don and Shirley Galloway Sr. My father, the late Rev. George Galloway Sr., was a civil rights freedom fighter and a leader. My father was a minister of the AME Methodist Organization from 1940 until 1992, when he passed. He was a man who truly loved God unconditionally. Rev. Galloway was a World War II veteran, minister of music, teacher of the Bible, and a graduate of A&T College and Selma University. My father, before his passing, was working on his book. It has been left up to myself and others to tell his story. The words my father used to name me, *the Freedom Baby*, only meant one thing, and that was to continue his legacy giving insight to who he truly was. I also want people to understand that, although he was a large part of my life, my story doesn't actually begin or end with my father's death; my journey must continue. I hope that reading his words and about his journey gives the reader inspiration, a continue of the fight for the people and that we all duplicate and use the tools that my father left behind to win and achieve a greater stepping-stone of achievements and lay out a path that will keep myself and others picking up that bravery fight for justice, equal rights, and equality.

Picture of the Late Rev. George Don Galloway.

Chapter 1
Changing Places

My father was born in Danville, Virginia, and raised in Washington, DC, with his mother and two other siblings. He graduated from Armstrong High School and pursued his baccalaureate studies at A&T College, Greensboro, North Carolina, with a concentration in music, arts, and history. He studied classical piano music. He serve in the United States Army for four years as a PFC and was a World War II veteran. He got out of the army returned back home to Washington, DC, and joined a local jazz band. Even though my father went to the army, he always found a piano. No matter where he was, he had the love for music; it was buried deep within his soul. He recalled one night playing in this Smokey nightclub in Newark, New Jersey. Its nickname was the Brick City because of the housing projects that were erected in the 1930s and 1940s. They were performing at this nightclub, and while on their break, an older woman spoke to him and told him that his purpose in life was to reach out to the people with the gift that God gave him not only with his music but with his wisdom of preaching God's words. She continued to ask him which church he attended, and he told her that he didn't have a church home and that he had just returned back home from the war. She went on to tell him that the church she attended was looking for a piano player and to come and visit her church and maybe speak with the choir director about the job. He took the information, contacted the choir director, and set up a meeting. He wasn't expecting to meet with a female. Her name was Mrs. White, an evangelist. He ended up playing for the church, and on one Sunday, the bishop of the church came for a visit. My father had an encounter with God, and he turned his life over to Christ that Sunday. He started studying the Bible under the studies of the bishop, and they became really close. My father started studying under the bishop at the Methodist Church, and he dedicated his life to studying theology. In the late 1940s, he was ordained to the Gospel Ministry in the African Methodist Episcopal Church in Washington, DC, and was later appointed as pastor of Mt. Calvary AME Church in Selma, Alabama, in 1954.

Rev. Galloway, could remember these days, as if,
it was yesterday, inside Brown Chapel, just one
of the meetings places for mass meeting.

Now moving from a large city into Selma, Alabama, where the blacks were not allowed to even sit and be served in a restaurant or able to walk on the same side of the sidewalk with white folks, was a big cultural shock. My father was very bright, a self-educated kind of man. He could talk to anyone about anything, so to come into this small town and look at what was happening, his radar went off as to things that needed to change in the South. In his first couple of months in Selma, he enrolled at Selma University, where he became associated with Rev. L. L. Anderson, the minister of Tabernacle Baptist Church. This man is the one who introduced my father to the movement, and my father became part of the Dallas County Voters League. The DCVL became the base for a group of activists who pursued voting rights and economic independence. Rev. L. L. Anderson opened up his church to the students for rally gathering because the church on Minter Street couldn't hold all the students, because after gathering during the day, for a while the number of students started growing, and they had to find a much larger place of meeting. Tabernacle church was located on one of the main arteries in town, which was on Broad Street. Only high school students were at the church everyday meeting. SNCC had not come to town yet to begin organizing the young folks. The student from Hudson High were organizing themselves on their own at this time. When the SNCC workers came to town, they started providing organization for the students and developed a strategy. The only problem with having the youths meet at Rev. Anderson's church was that the white people could see what was going when passing Tabernacle as they rode or walked down Broad Street. Mass meetings were moved from church to church. It finally came to the decision that First Baptist Church and Browns Chapel Methodist Church would become the central meeting place, mainly because these two churches were located in the heart of the black community. It was rare to see white people in that area. When the struggle for freedom began in the 1950s and early 1960s, my father would not have envisioned that he would have to come home from fighting in a war to participating in the civil rights movement and would culminate into one of the most heartrending civil wars of American History. Meanwhile, as my father gets settled more into his role in Selma and settling in at Mt. Calvary Methodist Church, he was asked by a church member at class one evening to run a revival at Peters and Chapel Church. Now this was a small church as well as a small town, and the members had heard from other churches about this preacher who could not only preach but could tear up a piano. This is the church where my father met my mother. My mother can recall having a best friend who liked Reverend Galloway.

My father was a very handsome distinguished man with curly low-cut wavy hair, beautiful light-brown skin, tall, and very well-spoken; and being a new young city man in a small town made him a very attractive prospect for a lot of single church women. My mother attended this church with her Grandma Mary, who happened to be a very God-loving, strict, firm woman raising my mother. My mother was a singer in the church. She would get up and lead a song and turn the church out. At age seventeen, she was not shy when it came to singing for the Lord. Her voice was of God's anointing. Word around town that a young musician and minister was holding a revival at Peters and Chapel and that he was truly a man who knew the word. Not only could he preach the word but could put a whipping on a piano. People talked about how he could play the piano like none had ever heard before, with the anointing that had you up singing and shouting. For the entire week, Reverend Galloway preached at the revival; and my great-grandmother Mary and her oldest daughter, Hester, and my mother did not miss a night. At this time, my mother and grandmother and Grandpa Davis were living in the country in a small town—Brantley, Alabama; and they traveled every night to the revival. My father started to have more conversations with Grandmother Mary. She was the head missionary and the mother of the church, and she made sure my father had a cold fresh pitcher of water up on the podium in the pulpit. It was one of her many tasks as the church mother. My father became close to Grandmother Mary and started to show interest in my mother, a beautiful young lady. She was Bishop I. H. Bonner's cousin. My father finally got up the nerve to ask Grandmother Mary if he could court my mother. He told my mother that he was nineteen, and my mother was seventeen. She only asked him about his age because she noticed that he had a streaks of gray running through his hair, but all in all, she believed him.

My mother was a young country girl living on a farm, working out in the fields. Having not much money and being a black female in a rural small town, she had a story to share with my father, especially since the way of living in the South was very different from where he came from. She was still in school. However, with the chores on the farm and the field work, an opportunity for education was slim to none. She had no brothers there to do the work. She had to help out. They dated for a year and got married in 1957 at a hall down in the bottom on the east side of Selma, across the Edmond Pettus Bridge. Bishop Anderson, whom my fathered studied under, married my mother and father. My mother wore a wedding gown that her grandmother made for her, and she looked beautiful in it. My father found a nice house and moved her grandmother with them to a house on Parkman Avenue in Selma. My mother—no stranger to hard work or keeping a clean house, ironing, sewing, or planting a garden in her own backyard—had all these crafts down to a science, considering that she was accustomed to this type of work living with her grandmother Mary. The only difference was that now she was in her own home, and she felt a lot more independent, and being that my father was older than her, he also helped her and guided her into becoming and knowing the role of first lady of the church and his wife. With more responsibilities now on my father, he wanted to provide more for my mother, and since he had moved into a house now, expenses were a lot more than when he was by himself, so he took a job working at a piano store for two blind men. They owned the music store and hired my father to sell and maintain and tune the piano in and out of the stores for many of the customers or churches that had purchased a piano from them. He started to teach piano lesson to the white kids in Selma, Lowndes, and Marion County. Strange you would think because these were white customers that my father had, and white folks would allow you into their homes to teach their kids piano lesson but didn't want to share the same side of the street with you. He also got a nighttime part-time job, cleaning the white folks' churches. And not to mention that he was still going to school at the university. But with all that he had going on, he still met with Reverend Anderson and the other DCVL group. Their goal was trying to register black citizens in Selma to have the right to be able to vote. My father, a man from the North, was definitely interested in getting involved with the movement because not only were his church members fighting this uphill battle of not being able to register and vote but his wife's family as well. So my father started attending the mass meeting more and really getting more involved as one of the leaders for this movement.

My father discussed with Reverend Anderson that he wanted to put together a civil rights choir. Well, everyone in town and the surrounding areas knew about my father and his minister of music, so it wasn't hard to find souls to be a part of this music movement. The audition took place at Browns Chapel. My dad didn't turn a soul away. He would not stop what God had for young souls who wanted to work for the Lord and for the cause. "Whoa, Freedom" was one of the first songs they started working on harmonizing, and my father's playing the piano made moments somewhat powerfully spiritual, and it made the song sound meaningful.

The red brick projects, or the G W. Carver Projects, were not only the backbone of the foot soldiers who tried to make a difference by fighting for social equality and justice but also for the folks, young and old, who lived there. My father knew how to get the movement fired up. He would break out in an old Gospel song like "God Is Not Dead. He's Still Alive," and that Browns Chapel Church wouldn't have a sitting soul. He would have everyone on their feet singing—praising and keeping the faith, knowing that God is still in control, even though Sheriff Clark thought he was in control. These foot soldiers were determined to march and get locked up, sometimes even beaten, on the streets for their rights. There were times when curfews were set in Selma, and my father would be on the streets going to check on the sick and shut-in members of his church, and some of Sheriff Clark's posse would try and harass my father, but he never wavered, and he knew that God was covering him, and they never laid a hand on him. My father would talk to many of the judiciary system—from the judges down to the clerks in the circuit court. He would talk about change. A lot of the men in the DCVL called my father crazy. They would tell him that he was putting his family and himself in danger by talking to those white folks that way, but my father knew his rights, and God was in control, and he thought that as long as he had God on his side, there was nothing to fear.

My father knew that some of the men he visited in their homes were part of the KKK. Most of the white folk who had either a pipe organ in their church or a piano in their house knew and would have Reverend Galloway come to their homes or churches either to tune a piano or give piano lessons, but my father was nobody's fool. He studied those white folks and knew who and what they were about, and the blind men who owned the piano shop definitely wasn't complaining because they were making money. My father would tell the deacons in his congregation and the men who were part of the movement and was worried that something was going to happen to him that "It may be time to deepen your spiritual roots. Change your spiritual influences. Just because you are religious doesn't mean that you don't need to update your faith intake. Sometimes our problem don't arise from the circumstances we predicted, the people we imagined, or the places we calculated. No matter how much we try and plan for trouble, you can never predict how long you will have to do battle or how hard." The second year into the marriage, my mother expected their first child, so my father wanted a larger house, and my mother's grandmother was still living with her, so they moved into a house on Small Street. Barely having time to spend at home with family and still going to university, ministering, participating in and helping organizing the movement, and working at the piano store, my father's plate was running over. He preached on Sundays at his own church and informed his church members as to what was going on and to ask if they would start attending the mass meeting. My father continued to keep going to the white churches to tune the piano, and he never stopped the piano lesson, because although there were a lot of the whites who were racists, there were also some who were not, and certain white families would let my father know if there was going to be trouble from the KKK or Sheriff Clark's posse.

Every day, my father and the DCVL would attempt to register blacks to vote, but the courthouse would either change the time of hours they could go register, or they would only allow a few at a time to be allowed to registered to vote. With music in his blood, every night at the mass meeting, he would always start off with a freedom song and had the choir to join in, and anytime they were gearing up to go and march down to that courthouse, that always got them in the mood for the battle they were about to face. The young protester would always leave the church after the meeting, singing from the top of their lungs "We Shall Overcome." My father got arrested several times. He recalled just sitting in the jail cell preaching to the young folks and singing freedom songs until they were release—songs like "Lift Every Voice and Sing." A lot of the foot soldiers didn't know this song, but by the time they were released, my father had taught that song to everybody in the cell. This rare and powerful combination of ministry of music and preaching God's word is something one just couldn't ignore. As he sat in that jail cell not knowing if or when he was going to be released or see his family, he couldn't let his faith get tested, so he kept his spirit and faith, and the young foot soldiers were uplifted as well by his preaching and singing. These young high school students who were placed in jail fighting for freedom to vote, equal rights, and justice were incarcerated for the determination of those in the civil rights movement in the face of government and social oppression. As they were sitting in that jail cell, one of the students said to my father that he was an adult whom everyone respected and his opinion meant a lot to the young foot soldiers. He also said to my father, "I'm proud to be involved with such a powerful movement, and we have all been praying and praying, but you are different … You want your answer right like now, and I think you brought the revolution to Selma right along with the rest of the men who fight hard every day to keep this movement alive."

As my father continued to fight for civil rights, my father's personal life with my mother was starting to be neglected and a bit harder than expected. On December 6, 1957, they had a baby girl, and on December 21, 1958, they had a baby boy. Of course, that only made things harder. I don't think my parents had considered how they would handle two babies. My mother was thankful to have the help of Grandma Mary. My mother never spoke poorly of my father, but sometimes, she said he was frugal and sometimes very tight with the money. If she said that the kids needed something like walking shoes, he would give only the exact cost down to the penny, not one dime over. They moved to a house on Sylvan Street, a nice black neighborhood, in a much larger house that had three bedrooms and one bathroom because the family was growing and much more room was needed. My mother started to work. She cleaned white folks' houses, and my great-grandma Mary would watch the kids while she went to work. She was such a great help. My father was gone a lot and busy with the civil rights movement; and since the county registration board opened doors for registration only two days out of the month or the personnel arrived late and took late lunches, it was very hard to pinpoint what time he would make it home after trying to get folks there to register to vote. The foot soldiers always had protest marchers day and night, and a lot of times, the sheriff deputies would block off a couple of streets before they could ever reached the courthouse. They got arrested every time they tried and went around the barricades to spend time in either the county jail, and when the county got full, Sheriff Clark would bus them to Camp Selma. This prison was fifteen miles southwest of Selma. They fed them white bread and syrup with pork and beans. The conditions were bad. All of the young adult and teenage foot soldiers were placed there overnight. My father can remember talking to the male students in the barracks with him. He told those strong young fighters that they were making a change and fighting for their rights was the only way and to not for one second even consider the situation they were actually facing at that particular time, with no bed, just a blanket and the hard floor, underneath their body—and that accomplishing the goal of what one believed in was well worth what they were enduring.

He was taken back to Selma that next morning by bus, and Sheriff Clarke had his way of hurting my father, and he had photographers on his payroll to take pictures of whoever decided to participate in the protest and took the photos to many of their employers, causing them to lose their jobs. My father was fired by the two blind men who owned the piano store. They let him come into work and gave him the orders they needed filled, and at the end of the workday, they asked him why he used the company van to haul around niggers to try to get them registered to vote. My father was thinking that he was not only carrying the young protesters to the east side to knock on doors to give them application to register to vote, but also he was carrying the supplies from Brown Chapel to the warehouse for the supplies he would distribute to the needy poor folks in Selma. He stood there in front of the two brothers and said to them that he used the van for the Lord's purpose. The oldest brother spoke to my father, demanding and giving him a choice to either stop protesting or they would have to let him go. He told my father that they were getting death threats, and they were told that they would burn down their business if they were to keep him employed. So my father took the van key off his key ring and handed it to the oldest brother and spoke to the both of them. He said, "If your rights were taken away from you only because the white man said it to be so and totally ignore the constitutional rights and not allow you to remain a first-class citizen, would you sit back and not fight? He then went on to tell the brothers that "Yes, I used your van trying to register and recruited as many as I could, and being threatened, attacked, beaten, and fired by you two is not going to make me not stand and fight for my freedom rights." The oldest brother reached out for my father's hand for a handshake, and my father shook his hand and said, "God is a forgiving God, so it's only righteousness that I live by that I forgive you too." He walked out the piano store and got in his car, wondering how was he going to tell his wife that he had lost his job. He said the verse in Matthew 6:25–34 out loud. My father then just let what had just happened to him release thru the wind. He knew he would be able to keep a lot of his clients of piano lesson and piano tuning because he was in high demand and was good at his craft, and the white folks knew they would not have to pay him as much as they would have to pay someone from another county. Since my father was no longer employed, the civil rights movement became his full-time job, and with his ministering at his church on Sunday, he picked up not only the leader of the civil rights choir, but he also was appointed head of supplies. Although he was already overseeing the supplies, he now had the time to take care of the inventory and distribute the supplies. He just had to figure out how he was going to tell his wife that he got fired!

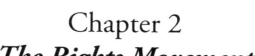

Chapter 2
The Rights Movement

It was a cold Sunday morning with the smell of homemade biscuits and baked chicken cooking in the oven. Three years had passed, and there was still struggle for the blacks to have the right to vote. Although the movement was alive and strong, it didn't feel much like the Civil Rights Act of 1957, and the constitutional protection of free assembly and speech was ever going to be something the blacks would conquer. My father was sitting in the dining room putting together his sermon for this morning. He was sitting there thinking even with the persistent work of SNCC and the Dallas County Voter League, it's almost impossible for African Americans to register to vote, especially with the registrar's office being open twice a month, on the first and third Monday, and potential applicants were routinely and arbitrarily rejected, even when some were well educated. Some were physically attacked, and others were fired from their job. This laid heavy on my father's mine, and he felt in his spirit that the sermon he needed to deliver this morning to his congregation was to speak on faith, that even when the fight looked like there was no way of winning, they must press on.

My mother wobbled through the living room, pregnant with the third child, to bring my father his pressed white button-down shirt to put on as he sat at the dining room table, waiting for breakfast to be served. He told my mom that "A change has to come. Selma has been fighting, and God won't put us up for this challenge to not let the outcome be a victory." As he ate his breakfast and my mother combed Barbara's hair, she told him, "We have to win not only for us but for our children and the next generation." My father echoed by saying, "Praise the Lord," as he finished up his breakfast. That morning at church, my father preached to his congregation about the problem of protesting from a fear point of view on he spoke on the times of conflict, chaos, confusion, discomfort, challenges, doubts, and fears as one pursues their destiny. "These feelings will not go away unless you learn to live with them. Move forward despite them, and trust God while you feel them. Waiting for your fears to subside, for conditions to be right, you will waste your life and never do what God called you to do, never pursue your destiny. The timing will never be perfect. Conditions will always be shaky. All the money you need may not be there. All the people you need may not be there, but you got to keep going. At every turn in your path to your destiny, walk with assurance that God will bring you through trouble, through confusion, through disappointment.

"The choices of either living with the threat of failure or live forever as a slave to fear. It's not what you go through that matters. It's what you feel about what you go through." As my father spoke to his congregation, he knew that this fight for freedom must continue, and he ensured them that they must never give in or give up. When church service came to a close, he felt that he had reached the members who were active in the movement and making his point known that we can't let these white folks win and nor turn us around. As Monday came, my father worked alongside others trying to get the blacks registered to vote. He helped SNCC youth organizations to go door-to-door with applications to get blacks in Selma registered to vote with not much success and with many protest marches and many mass meeting about trying to organize a successful way to overcome and win the rights for many blacks to have the opportunity to register to vote, but with the city courthouse making the law of a verbal registration, that made it difficult to register to vote. Being arrested for protesting many times and after being placed with many other protesters in the county jail before he and others were released, they were warned by the authorities to stop protesting. The crowd got too large to place all the protester in the local county jail, and my father kept protesting trying to get blacks registered to vote. The court and the chief of police Sheriff Clark created and set up Camp

Selma, a large prison camp where they would bus the protestor and detain them. The routine normally was they kept my father detained overnight and release the next day. They always had four and five buses available especially when all the women and children and the students would protest. These marches were only held at sudden times, when the marchers marched to the courthouse to register, my father and the organization only used the adults to march. My father can remember one of the times they had a large march and Sheriff Clarke had the buses to come and take them away. He remembered when they loaded the buses this time, and there were so many protesters they filled every seat, and once all seats were filled, the first person standing was instructed to move all the way to the back of the bus, and a line started for those who were standing, including my father, who was standing in the middle of the aisle, which was filled from the back to the front of the bus; and this young woman was standing on the bottom step of the bus, and another young woman was standing next to the bus driver. The deputy was standing at the door of the bus, trying to push the young lady up the stairs so that the bus doors could swing close, so when he asked the young lady to move up the stairs, there was no more room to go anywhere. The bus was full to capacity. The deputy took the cattle prod and electric shocked this young lady so badly that her eyes rolled back into her head, and everyone started to push toward the back so that the young lady that was standing by the bus driver could help the young lady off the steps. She was deranged because of the shock. My father recalled just starting to pray out loud, asking God to forgive them. There were two people from him to the young ladies, and he started to reach out his hands to them and prayed to God for protection and to cover and protect them. The bus driver told my father that he would call the deputy back over to his bus if he didn't stop the noise. Imagine that he called praying noise. My father was standing next to a young teenage boy who had a community newspaper. He must have been one of the black young teenagers who sold the paper. He took the newspaper and began to fan the young lady so she could get some air, because they were so packed on that bus; it was no type of circulation. He looked around on that bus and saw men and mostly Hudson High school students, and he thought these students were keeping the struggle of the phase alive. But even taking these students to prison camp didn't strike fear within them. The bus took them to camp Selma, and they placed them in the barracks. The conditions were a lot tougher there than in the county jail. There wasn't any water or food for them, and my father and many others were abused with the cattle prods.

There was one urinal and one sink in this particular holding cell, and they placed my father and the other men together and the women in another holding cell. It was like an open room with no window just a large open jail cell with flatbed mattresses on the floor with no cover, not a lot of room to move around because it was like 150 people in one holding cell together, and they talked and made plans at camp Selma having their own mass meeting on how they would continue on even after their release. They discussed and held training sessions about how to remain peaceful while protesting and how to protect yourself if they were attacked. They also sang freedom songs to pass the time, not knowing when they would be released; they just continue to pray. Camp Selma was a prison for the chain gang that went out every day, and my father could look out that square window to the outside yard, and my father can remember telling himself, "If these white folks keep me there and place us on the line to work with the prisoners, I'm going to kneel and refuse." He was willing to give his life for his First Amendment rights, and with him born and raised in the North, he knew what his rights were and was not going to have them just taken away. After five long days and nights, they were taken back to Selma and released. When my father walked into the house, my mother asked him what happened and proceeded to tell him that many of the congregation was looking for him. She didn't know if he was dead or beaten and couldn't help himself. She was so shaken up but in the same breath happy and thankful he was safe and alive. My father was more than happy to be home, but he knew he had to continue on. No matter how many times he could get arrested, he was going right back out there and fight. His copastor got word that he had made it home, and he came over along with the deacon of my father's church, and they had a meeting that night, strategizing how they could take care of each other family if any one of them got arrested. My father shared with them about Camp Selma and the conditions and warned them if the county jail was to get filled up, they would most likely be bus to Camp Selma. As they were sitting and having their meeting, my mom started to bring to the dining table a plate full of fried pork chops smothered with gravy, fried tomatoes, mashed potatoes, plus the vegetables. She knew this meal would satisfy my father, especially after being placed in that prison with barely much to eat. She knew this was surely a meal he would greatly appreciate. My father said the grace, and the men at the table with my father went in on that meal; you would have thought that they were incarcerated with my father. The work of my father on the black-led civil rights movement was the most momentous social struggle in postwar America. It was a second American revolution. The civil rights movement marched our democracy up to a new plateau.

In 1961, the population of Dallas County was 57 percent black, but of the 15,000 blacks old enough to vote, only 130 were registered—fewer than 1 percent. At that time, more than 80 percent of Dallas County blacks lived below the poverty line, most of them working as sharecroppers, farmhands, maids, janitors, and day laborers; but there were also teachers and business owners. With the literacy test administered subjectively by white register, even the educated blacks were prevented from registering or voting, so my father said at one of the mass meetings Rev. Reese, the Boyntons, and other DCVL members decided to help gather up teachers, and Rev. Reese put together some questions and held citizenship school classes focused on the literacy test required for voter registration and canvassed door-to-door, encouraging African Americans to come and attend and get the help to prepare themselves for the questions that just might be asked when they try and register. My father studied, and he passed and was registered to vote. He was basically tried to register in Selma because he had been up North and was registered to vote, and he could not understand why was it that the white folks felt the need to try and stop them from voting when they had every right as any other American citizen. They even went as far as Wilcox and

Lowndes counties, letting them know about the classes. There were virtually no blacks on the voting rolls in these rural counties that were roughly 80 percent black. And to think that more than 100 percent of the eligible white population was registered, and this was why SNCC and the DCVL organizing was necessary and extremely challenging because African Americans in Selma, despite being a majority in the community, were systematically disfranchised by the white elite who used literacy tests, economic intimidation, and violence to maintain the status quo. White terrorism created a climate of fear that impeded organizing efforts, and my father and other African Americans were not going to be threatened nor defeated or prevented from accessing their constitutional right to vote. My father, being very active in the movement, was assigned to several jobs at Browns Chapel unlike some of the others. He now worked for himself and had the free time to be available almost always. He organized and directed a civil rights choir, and my mother's cousins, the Houser sisters, were a group that lead the choir. He was head of the Selma visitors and security putting together a security detail schedule of overnight watchmen to keep Browns Chapel from being bombed. The one project that was important to him, and he basically thought the federal food relief program was very important. This program was set up to keep thousands of seasonally employed black farmers from starvation and helped to clothe and feed the Southern rural poverty people. My father was also policing them and mobilizing the black community gaining their trust by providing food and clothing alone with political information and organization.

Field secretary taught the political relationship between starving children and unregistered parents, making it clear that he was willing to help those who would help themselves onto the rolls of registered voters. Instead of two or three, now scores of blacks were attending mass meetings and were gathering at the courthouse to register. My father also worked with the young Hudson High School students and young adults at the mass meeting, training them how to provoke any violence, even though the violence that was placed upon them with the racial white violence and white repression in Selma was systematic and long-standing. Selma was home to Sheriff Jim

Clark, a violent racist, and one of Alabama's strongest white citizens councils made up of the community's white elite and dedicated to preserving segregation and white supremacy. The threat of violence and retaliation was so strong that most African Americans were afraid to attend a mass meeting. Most of the first recruits to stand beside my father and others were high school students, and this was why my father thought that the federal food relief program was so important to have in place, because if some of the adults were to get fired from their job, there was still a program set up to at least give those families food and clothing and personal supplies to help them until they could find employment elsewhere. My father made it known to the young students because even though they were too young to vote, they canvassed and taught classes to adults helping them with studying for the Alabama literacy test. Selma was so brutal my father can recall encouraging attendance at a mass meeting in May 1963. The Lafayettes combined a memorial service for Mr. Boynton with a voting workshop and rally. SNCC leader spoke to the large crowd of over three hundred people. The whites tried their best to intimidate. They gathered around the church, yelling out threats that they were going to burn all the niggers inside the church together, and they walked around the church yelling out threats. And since they already knew that Sheriff Clark and other local lawmen were basically would not do anything to have those men removed from around the church, my father started to play the piano, and the church started to singing freedom songs to bolster their courage until 1:00 a.m., and finally the armed crowd dispersed.

Rev. Galloway, had many responsibilities, but, the
leader, of the Civil Rights chorus was special.

My father set up for two watchmen to stay around the church
until daybreak because the KKK were already putting out the word
that they would bomb any church that had any rallies or meetings.
Some of the men thought that it wasn't necessary to set up security,
but my father said to them, "We don't know if they would bomb it
or not. It's a classic don't-know situation," and he went on to say, "I
have frequently found that someone hunches a lot of times are more
of an accurate view of reality than one's knowledge. But if I act on
your thinking or hunch, then I bear all the responsibility for the outcome, not you." So, of course, there is no winning your point across

my father when he was committed to the job at hand, especially with him feeling like he was responsible for taking care and making sure the church was safe and not destroyed. So after my father set up the watchmen, it was about a quarter past one, and my father made it home and couldn't sleep sitting at the dining room table. There was nothing much to eat all day since the bacon sandwich from this morning, and he began to pray and talk to God, asking him to build a fence around all his black brothers churches. He meditated in the word in prayer and went to bed. A couple of months after that frightful night, the groups thought it was time for a large march. This type of march included the younger children, women, and the high school students combined. They started from Browns Chapel and headed to the courthouse, walking side by side on the sidewalks to stay within the ordinance so as not obstruct traffic. As they approached the courthouse, Sheriff Clark and his lawmen were blocking the road and instructed everybody to get on the buses they had parked on the street in front of the courthouse. The younger children and some of the women turned backed, and my father and other leaders loaded on the buses and was taken to the National Guard Amory in Selma. My father stayed there for about five hours. Then they loaded us back on the buses, thinking they were taking us back to Camp Selma. But instead, they took us to another camp called Camp Thompson. This place was a large building concrete walls with long hallways with barracks built onto it.

These barracks were numbered and were like open dormitory-style housing. As my father walked down these halls, there were barracks 1 and barracks 2. All the heat was in the hallway. As they took them to the barracks, my father remembered it being really cold, and there was no heat once you left the hallway and were placed into the barracks. They took turns and went to a screen where you could feel the heater blowing, which was basically how they stayed warm. Male and females were separated. They fed them well the first night. However, after they learned who they were. They were fed beans the rest of the time just like the prisoner. They were held at Camp Thompson for seven long days. They did not wash during this time. They were not permitted to wash. After the seventh day, they were taken back to Selma for a court hearing. My dad was charged with unlawful assembly. He remembered the judge coming out of his chambers and sniffing the air like an animal as he prepared to enter the room. The judge turned around, went back into his chambers, came back into the courtroom with a can of air freshener, and sprayed the courtroom. None of them were given the chance to shower or even wash off for seven days. They were numb to the smell. My father had a thought back to when he was serving in the army and used to go out in the fields for training, and he could recall smelling a whole lot better living in the woods than living in that prison, and to have your freedom taken away and being treated like you were not a citizen of this country was mind-blowing, and to know that you fought for this country only made him more determined to keep pushing forward and let none of this resistance stop him. It was a joyful day to get to take a long hot shower and get a good hot meal before he started back up on getting right back where he left off. My mother didn't give him grief about the time. He wasn't spending at home, and she didn't give him grief for taking Barbara and George with him now that they were old enough to go with him to attend the mass meeting. He took them with him to help with sorting out the federal supplies at the warehouse. George would help him load the supplies in the station wagon at Brown Chapel, and they then would go to the warehouse and sort. They were a lot of help to my father and was glad to be a part of this powerful movement. My mother was not critical to the movement's success in Selma. She knew sacrifices had to be made. Like their male counterparts, they also organized, demonstrated, taught, preached, and strategized.

They also cooked and housed workers, tried to register, and recruited friends and neighbors. And like the men, they were threatened, attacked, beaten, and fired. Through it all, they stood up for themselves and their communities, insisting on their freedom rights. They all put their bodies on the line to demand these rights and refused to back down in the face of violence. That's why they joined hands to work alongside their husbands organizing around voter registration and community empowerment. Winter was here again. Leaves were gone off the trees, and it was another season was among them, and nothing was changed, but the fight was still strong and mighty. On September 15, 1963, was a sad day for the black community. The bombing of the church in Birmingham, Alabama, sent a sadness that was hard to describe. My father decided to go to Birmingham on that Monday with Reverend Shannon and Rev. L. L. Anderson. They went to Birmingham to a meeting after the four black girls attending Sunday school were killed when a bomb exploded at the Sixteenth Street Baptist Church, a popular location for civil rights meeting in Birmingham, Alabama. And since my father was over the security detail at Browns Chapel, they not only went for support but to also see what the report stated as to how they planted the bombs and what explosive they used and what signs to look for to prevent anything like this to happen at Browns Chapel. When my father returned back to Selma that Monday evening, he held another deliverance day of prayer on that Tuesday, pretty much like the one they had back a couple of years ago when the bus boycott was going on. My father and sister Mattie Moss's church in east Selma joined my father, and they both kept their church doors open for prayer and support to anyone who was having doubt or just felt like giving up especially after what happened to the little girls in Birmingham. Many people were afraid, and with Selma being such a brutal town already—with the whites being so cruel and dangerous—people were afraid. So my father felt that this was necessary to keep the hope and faith alive. A lot of parents were worried about their children more since this incident, and they knew that white folks didn't have a problem killing any of them. This was a very hard and sad time. My father's commitment to the struggle was something he took to heart. It was all at the risk of life and limb and injury. He wanted his people to know that God fills us with the strength and courage to stay within his word and have faith and not be afraid if we continue to trust and believe that God is our protector, and we must continue to walk with God, and our prayers will be answered. Prayer moves mountains, and this was why he called for the deliverance day of prayer. The KKK was not going to place fear and cause them to quit. My mother and her family was frightened for his life, but she knew and trusted that God would cover them all. That's the type of faith you had to have in order to maintain and stand your ground. He defied the white powers who sought to keep blacks oppressed. His fight for the right to earn a fair wage, equality in education, the right to elect leaders, and other basic freedoms made him a true warrior and a determined civil rights fighter. My father always said that he came from the North and had all the rights, and he exercised his rights, and this is why he said he had to defend and restore the rights of mankind given to us by the United States of America's Constitution standing strongly against the injustices and the Jim Crow Laws of the South. A couple of weeks passed, and my father was at Paul's Episcopal Church tuning the pipe organ and was approached by one of the white men who let my father in the church. He began his conversation, telling him that the judge whose children received piano lessons from him too was offering from the justice department to clear up his records and he was willing to drop all injunctions and leveled against him and the other men who were leaders like the courageous eight and other if they would stop the protesting. My father quickly and firmly told the young white male that only death would stop him. My father knew that the other men were unified and had the same goals for the Selma community. He then continued to tell him that we wouldn't stop marching, stop boycotting, and stop demonstrating at lunch counters in this segregated business and streets of Selma until they were treated fairly. He said, "I fought for this country and will not stand by and let my freedom be taken away." He stood up from tuning the organ, and he looked at the white man's face and said, "My freedom was not free, and the struggle continues every day," and then he asked him, "Have you ever had to fight to get back something that was yours and should not have been taken away in the first place?" The white guy didn't answer. He just stared back at my father, and then my father said, "All these legal barriers and the so-called literacy test, terrorism, economic retaliation, and police harassment only make me fight for the cause even more." The white man walked off, and my father went back to working on the pipe organ and left there feeling that he didn't take selling out on this union of men lightly. He told L. L. Anderson about the conversation later that night when they met for a mass meeting. October 7, 1963 was called Freedom Day. This day was organized with it being one of the monthly registration days. James Baldwin and Dick Gregory were in town in Selma as supporters letting the blacks know that they were not alone.

On this bright crisp cool day, over three hundred African Americans stood in line to register, but the registrar processed only forty applications, and white lawmen refused to allow people to leave the line to go to the restroom and return. The lawman arrested the SNCC workers standing on federal property holding signs promoting voter registration. Many elderly waited in the hot sun, and they all started to get concerned for the elderly standing ever since in the morning in this long line, and it was then midafternoon. So the men who were part of the organization gathered up money to go and collect sandwiches from Lannie's restaurant and water. As the two men were approaching the crowds with the water and sandwiches, they were beaten by the highway patrolmen and arrested. The FBI agents and two justice department attorneys refused to intervene. It was a shame that the Southern white officials persistently and openly defied both the civil rights acts of 1957 and constitutional protections of free assembly and speech; and the FBI claimed to have no authority to intervene, because the matters were local police matters, but they consistently ignored such constraints to arrest others violating federal law. As the evening went on and the courthouse closed for business, the line stayed long and strong until the workers who worked at the courthouse came out to go home. The crowd broke up, and everyone went home. Although there were not many who got a chance to register, they still stood strong outside the courthouse to make that statement that they would register if not all but at least some. That same evening, a mass meeting was held at the Browns Chapel Church to discuss that odays situation and to plan for the more protest. By 8:00 p.m., nearly three hundred people were wedged shoulder to shoulder inside the church, with many gathered outside in the chilly darkness to hear songs and speeches and prayers broadcast through speakers they made so the people on the outside could hear as well. Dick Gregory was in the church, and he spoke to us letting us know to fight the fight and that he was with Selma. My father played that piano with folks singing and shouting and praising with sweat beads rolling off his face with the Holy Spirit moving through that church with every one being up lifted with courage and the will to keep the movement alive.

Rev Galloway, and other protesters waiting in line to try to register to vote in Selma Alabama (noted as freedom day)

Chapter 3
When School Was Cruel

The school year began in August 1964. The three oldest children—Barbara, nine, George, eight, and Patsy six—were attending an all-black school, Payne Elementary School. The school was not integrated, and they didn't even have textbooks. My siblings remembered the school as not having a library with many books and a lot of thin paperback books. Most of the books that were in decent condition were shared. The family had expanded over the years. There was a four-year-old baby girl named Bernice at home with my mother, and she was pregnant with the fifth child on the way. Mother's grandmother would stay over sometimes to help out, so my father moved the family to 1427 St. Phillip Street to have a little bit more room. My mother, being a great seamstress, she made all the clothes for the kids and herself as well. By this time, my father was very much involved with the movement, even after being jailed numerous times for either marching without a permit or standing out in front of the courthouse with many of his own church members and family members trying to register to vote. My mother and grandmother were active and participated in marches sometimes, and my father would always take George and Barbara with him to all the mass meetings, and they would sit with some of the older ladies while Daddy played the piano and the civil rights choir song freedom songs. And after they finished worshipping, he met with the other DCVL organizers. George and Barbara talked about how mother would prepare meals for the meetings that occurred at our home on St. Phillip Street. Those men would come to the house with top hats with nice pressed suits and long overcoats sitting down at the dining room table to have a meeting. Barbara told us that when the meetings happened, Mother would tell them to go to their room, but she and George were so pumped from being involved with the mass meetings at the church until they didn't want to miss out on whatever the men were talking about. George talked about when they would protest with the marchers. He remembered the sounds of shoes hitting the pavement and holding hands with his mom, he on one side and his great-grandmother Mary on the other side. As they were walking, someone stepped on the back of his shoe because he was taking smaller steps, so he had to skip and hop to keep up. They marched side by side, holding hands and singing freedom songs. He thought he was in a parade, not being quite old enough to understand what all the marching was about, he took in the adventure and excitement not even knowing that he would one day come to know when he became a man that he participated in the march on freedom civil rights movement. By the end of 1963 going into 1964, my father was appointed to Peters and Chapel Church a small church in Selma, and he was the assigned pastor at another church in Atlanta, Georgia, named Pleasant Hill Church. He was no longer the minister at Mt. Calvary and no longer working at the piano store. With the completion of college at Selma University and with the family growing bigger, he took on these two churches to take care of his family, and he refused to work for the white man ever again, especially after the way he was treated. He felt that when that white man asked him to not stand for what he believed in and was trying to make him choose a paycheck over his freedom, my father would always tell my older siblings that "Nothing is worth your First Amendment Rights" and to "Never let no one talk you out of your freedom to exercise your freedom of speech and equality." The education problem with the segregation of school laid heavy on his mind, although he knew the black schools were doing the best they could; but when he saw how his kids barely had school books and the condition of the books were really not books, he thought back to where he went to school up North and had the opportunity to have the tools to learn with great learning literature and school supplies. He just felt like something needed to be done. Schools were supposed to become integrated in

September 1963, and this was a crucial time for all the black kids in the South; and with my father being a big supporter on education, he would discuss with Mr. Reese, the president of the DCVL and also a teacher at Hudson High School, about doing something about the education for our children because my father felt that they deserved the best of education just like the white kids. When the segregation law passed and black kids were attempting to go to the white schools, my father took quickly to the streets and going door-to-door to every African American home and talking with the parents and trying to convince them to go with him to school superintendent office to register their kids to attend the white schools. He went to many of the leaders who had a strong impact on the movement and the people asking them to help him convince everyone to go as a unified group to integrate the Selma school, but they declined, afraid of putting their children in harm's way. So with all the negative talk about my father, that he was crazy to put his children in danger, they said that he was committing a foolish act. With no one by his side, he met with the school superintendent and the school board of Selma on that Friday. Meeting with a white staff of racist people, my father refused to let them intimidate him or make him feel or his children feel as if they didn't deserve the best education just like the white kids. So that Friday morning, he enrolled his kids at the Baker Elementary School. Now the whites were not going to let it be easy for my father to accomplish his goal. They told my father that his kids would have to take a placement test to see if his children could pass an equivalence test and in order to attend the school they would have to pass. There was no study material given to my father for my siblings to study, so my father worked with the three kids and prepared them for the test. Barbara helped her younger siblings study. She was very smart academically. Word got out that my father had registered his kids, and the KKK came through my parents' neighborhood late at night, driving slowly by the house while yelling out racist slurs, threatening that they would not allow any niggers to go to school with their kids. Threats came that entire weekend, and my mother was scared for her entire family. She had her relatives and neighbors telling her to not send her kids to that white school; but my father, being the stubborn and determined man that he was, he was not going to give in to the whites or my mother. On Sunday, my father preached about what God was telling him to do as for as placing his kids at the white school the next day after that, and he prayed about it, and he left everything in God's hands. Fearing no man, he just had that strong faith to believe that they would be protected when they walked on the school grounds the day after. Mother normally wouldn't disagree with him nor try and convince him, but she told him that night as she was preparing the children clothes for school, she said to my dad that if anything should happen to her children, she would make him wish he had never sent them to that school. It was a cool Monday morning, and my mom prepared oatmeal for them to eat before school. After they finished their breakfast, they prayed at the table, and they headed to school. Barbara and Diane's hair were pressed and tied into two ponytails and with front bangs; beautiful ribbons draped on the end of their ponytails. They had on beautiful printed dresses that my mother made for them with baby doll socks and patent leather shoes. George had a fresh haircut and plaid stripe shirt with freshly ironed slacks with nice hard bottom shoes. They were definitely the best-dressed kids who would be attending that school that day, and my parents spared nothing when it came to making sure that the kids had the finer things in life. My mother was a seamstress. It was nothing for her to pull out a pattern, go and purchase some beautiful material from the fabric store, and make the kids some unique pieces to wear. The neighbors always thought of Barbara as a walking baby doll because of the way my mother dressed her. There were two sisters by the name Naydeen and Phyllis, preteens. They were neighbors, and their mother would babysit the kids whenever Mother worked and my great-grandmother wasn't available, and they always enjoyed walking the girls up and down the sidewalk, stating that Barbara was their baby doll, and they always complimented on how the kids always were dressed to the nine. And that morning, as those sisters were leaving to attend their school, my father was loading my siblings in the car to head to the new school. My siblings really didn't feel nervous, although they didn't know how they would feel going to school with white kids when they didn't even want to be on the same side of the sidewalk with blacks, so you know the white kids definitely didn't want to share the classroom with them. When my father drove them up to the school, the lawman and white parents were standing in front of the school and telling them to "Go back to your nigger school. We don't want your kids at our school." They were spitting and yelling out, making mean gestures as they were approaching the stairs. My father walked them through the angry white crowd and entered the school. They went to the principal's office, and my dad signed them in. There was a white woman who came up to my father and told him that his children needed to go with her to take the placement test. Barbara remembered going into a room with nothing but white folks present. The white teacher put the test in front of her and told her to take the test. She had no idea what the test was about, but she did study with her dad and was not sure if what they had studied would even be on the test.

She did exactly what the teacher advised her to do. When she completed the test, she was escorted back to the front office where she saw her father and siblings waiting for her. As they sat waiting, there were white parents coming into the school, walking past the principal's office and yelling out racist gestures, but my father paid them no mind and told my siblings that they had every right to be there just as much as their kids. After sitting in the office for almost thirty minutes, the principal and three teachers approached my father and siblings and spoke with my father. The principal told my father that Barbara passed the test with a 100 average score, and not only was she ready to attend the white folks school; her learning abilities and the level on how well she tested and comprehended called for her to be double promoted. She was placed in the third grade. Her siblings did not take the placement test with the way the white folks mind's think. They were convinced by the way Barbara passed her test. They assumed that the other kids didn't needed to be tested, and the two other siblings were placed in their assigned classroom with no problem. Barbara had no problem mixing in with the white students on their first day of school. She became really close friends to a white girl who sat next to her in class. They shared homework together, and she was her only playmate at school. George, on the other hand, had a rocky start. He didn't make any friends at first. He basically went in the classroom doing the best he could considering the teacher was very racist and she was grading George *un*fairly because of the color of his skin. One day, as he attended his history class, the subject of the lesson that day was Africa. The teacher pointed out to the other students in the classroom that George being black and how he arrived here in the United States from Africa. Now George sat there thinking, "I came from Africa," and thinking, "I have never been to Africa." As the teacher continued to explain to the students that George was African who came from Africa and used to live in the jungle with the wild animals, George thought, "I will ask my dad about this when he gets home," and he did just that. As the family was sitting down for dinner, George told my father what the teacher said to him, and my father was furious. He explained to George that he has never seen Africa. My father then got up from the table and walked over to his study bookshelf, which had about twenty books plus the encyclopedias and pulled from the shelf a black-and-white history book and the geology map of the world, and he explained to George and showed him where Africa was located and went over the history of how the blacks in Africa were kidnapped and brought over in chains to the United States of America against their own will, to be placed at slave owners' land to work for free and work for the white men.

He was furious at the information the teacher was giving to the white students. Not only was it inaccurate, but it was racial also. He told George that he would be joining him in his classroom tomorrow to address this matter. My father knew the cruelty of how the white folks could be toward him as an adult, and he knew he would never allow his children to be placed in such a unfairly treatment environment and he not take a stand and let his son know that he would never be told anything, and he believed it to be true about himself, and never would he let this white teacher to win and place such untruth upon his son. The next morning, as the kids prepared themselves for school and finished their oatmeal, my father took them to school, still facing some of the still angry parents who still didn't want them attending the school. They briskly walked past the angry, loud white parents. My father told my siblings to go on to class. As they proceeded to their assigned classroom, my father went into the principal's office. He stood there in the office for about five minutes and was ignored, so he started to walk to the principal's door, and the white secretary looked up over her glasses, pretending that she was shuffling papers, and she spoke to my father, telling him he couldn't go into the principal's office and that he was not in his office yet. So my father told the secretary that he needed to speak with him. She then asked my father if he had an appointment. My father said in an authoritarian way that he didn't need an appointment to speak to the principal when it was a matter pertaining to one of his teachers. He sat patiently waiting, and the principal walked into the office, and my father got up and approached the principal with a "Good morning" and a handshake. Well, my father already knew that this principal would rather eat nails than to have to deal with him, but my father was not going anywhere until he got his point heard. He followed the principal inside his office, and he told him about the incident that happened yesterday with George and his teacher. My father requested to have the principal to escort him to George's class-room. As they walked down the hallway silently with class in session, they approached George's classroom, and the principal walked into the classroom in front of my father, and he explained that my father was a minister and wanted to speak to the class, more of setting it up as if my father was a guest. My father stood in front of George's class, introduced himself to the classroom full of white kids, and greeted the teacher. My father started off with saying, "Greetings in the precious name of Jesus, who is the head of my life and truly my redeemer and whom I am satisfied to be mine for he bought us with a price that no man could pay but sin. I am happy to stand here and tell you students and the teacher that I am saved. Leaning and depending on Jesus. You see, my son makes my day. The Lord is good to have given him to be with me in the flesh and the spirit. Other than God, he is my sunshine and joy as if you are your parents' joy. Therefore, we thank and praise his holy name, thanking God for a son with a meek spirit with a pure innocent heart. I tell all my children through

Christ Jesus, you can do all things, knowing about whence you have come and how he has been trained thus far to stage in his life and knowing about the experience at such a young age as to where he came from, and I can assure you that he did not come from Africa climbing trees like a monkey. I am grateful to our heavenly Father to give me the knowledge to help everyone in this classroom know that we are one and we all come from the same place." My father then walked over to the teacher standing in the corner of the classroom and said to her charge, "Thee, therefore, God and the Lord Jesus Christ, who shall judge the quick and the dead at his appearing and his kingdom. Teach the truth to your sheep. Preach the word." He then quoted the 2 Timothy 4:1–2, and he opened the door with the teacher looking at my father with tears in her eyes, and the principal, lost for words, walked out.

As the principal and my father walked down the hall back to his office, my father continued to walk on out of the school without another word said between the two men. George came home that evening and told the other siblings what happened at school and that the teacher apologized to him, and from that day on, the teacher taught his class on a Bible study class level and was a different teacher. Although George always got the dogs seek on him every day after school at least, he felt like his father was his hero at least for that day. The third child, Diane, who started at the school had her little mishap with one of the white students. This sibling was a very quiet and was pretty much a loner because the kids in her classroom were very mean and were taught since kindergarten to be racial toward blacks and didn't know any better. One morning, as school started and the students were in first period, Diane sat in the back of the class mainly because the students really didn't want her there, but Diane paid no mind. She was so excited to see the new fresh books and workbooks that she basically ignored the students and their mean gestures toward her. As first period got underway and went to sit down in her chair without her noticing a white girl behind her, she proceeded to sit in her chair. The little white girl pulled Diane's chair out from under her, and Diane went falling facefirst into the desk, gashing the side close to her temple open. Blood was gushing, and the little girl panicked and started screaming and with the blood running down my sister's face. The teacher quickly approached her with a cloth that she collected out of her desk holding the cloth and escorting my sister to the principal's office. She did not take her to the school nurse because white nurses did not medically care for the blacks. There was no black nurse at the school working, so she went into the principal's office and told the secretary to call my parents to pick her up to take her to the black hospital for medical care. Diane was very calm, and the teacher instructed my sister to wait in the office that her parents were on the way to get her. My mother was at home, and the telephone rang, and the school told her about the accident but didn't tell her what really happened. My father was still at the house. He hadn't left for work yet. They jumped in the car and rushed to the school, and as soon as they opened up the principal's office door, there was Diane sitting there with the bloody cloth, holding it to her head. My father picked her up, and they took her to the hospital, and they stitched up her very deep gash and was told that she was blessed that she didn't hit her temple, or it could have been deadly. When the doctor was telling my parents of the seriousness the fall could have been, Diane quickly interrupted and said she didn't fall, the white girl pulled the chair out from under her, and the teacher watched her do it. My parents were furious. My mother insisted that they not go back to that school; it was too dangerous, but my father told my mother that life was going to be rough and throw them into situations that they had to deal with even at the early years of their lives. My mother totally disagreed with my father, but she knew there was no changing his mind of pulling them out of the white school. That evening, when school let out, my father was sitting outside the school, waiting for Barbara and George, and he explained to them what happened to Diane and that being violent and retaliating is not the answer, the way to beat these white folks at the cruelness is to stay and attend the school, keep studying hard, maintain good grades, and overall we win. He said to them that love conquers all.

As they left the school, they went to Browns Chapel to pick up the supplies that had been delivered to the church. They loaded the car with all the supplies and went to the warehouse they had set up to store all the stuff, and once they arrived at the warehouse, my father did inventory on the new supplies, and then George and Barbara helped him load the supplies in the car, and they went to the family in need and distribute the items. When my father went to these families, he would talk and pray with these families. A lot of them were poor and was trying to make it. Some of them lost work due to trying to register to vote. Some were misplaced and taken out of homes that they were renting from white landlords. Some of the farmers were cut off from getting the supplies to harvest all due to these black folks in Selma Alabama and abroad in the rural counties outside of Dallas County being punished only because they knew how important the power of your voices being heard meant for us as a black community and our future. Change would never come for the blacks if we didn't have the right to vote. It would be like being nonexistent in this world and no future for the ones left behind them. The clothing and food that my father issued out to these families, and many of them that he ministered to needed the encouraging words the many prayers and positive talk of keeping the faith and not be afraid and not giving up. Truth be told, it was not an easy task. Most of the people in Selma had been either threatened or were physically harmed. There were many times my father were threatened, and cross burning went on in front of many homes including our own, and white knight riders kept looking to harm any blacks that they saw, especially those who were just leaving the mass meetings. Mass meetings always let out at night, mostly late at night, and my father was followed many of nights by trucks with bright lights shining into his car, almost blinding his view, and white men standing on the back of the truck followed him home after mass meetings. We asked our father why was he not afraid and why they never attacked him, and he would answer us saying that "God places the courage of a lion in your heart, and you have the faith to know that what I'm fighting for are the rights of my children and many others even when I am dead and gone, and all my sacrifices would be well worth it." George often thought all the time that his dad had powers that no one could touch him, because he remembered the one time it was his birthday. My mother made a cake, and Selma was placed on a curfew, and blacks could not be out after a certain time at night in Selma, and he wanted that chocolate ice cream to go with his chocolate cake mother baked for his birthday. So what did my father do? They were living on St. Phillip Street at the time. Instead of my father driving to the store, he and George walked to the store and purchased the ice cream, and on their way back home, a car followed them. My father never picked up his pace, and he didn't seem afraid. The car pulled slowly up beside them, and my dad looked right into those white men's faces inside the car with their interior light on so you could see them and George said him and my father just kept walking.

The car accelerated and drove off, speeding into the dark. They made it back home safely. Another incident that George experienced with my father—and he still questions the situations today and can't understand how his father made it out of the civil rights movement alive—was on a Saturday when my father cleaned some of the white folks churches there in Selma—the same churches whose pianos he maintained and kept tuned. On this particular day, George and my father were cleaning the church, and they were carrying the trash bags out of the church, loading them into the car to take to the land-fill, when this white member from the church approached George and told him to carry the crates he had on the back of his truck inside the dining hall of the church. Well, that didn't go off too well with my father. My father walked over to the white man and told him that "My son does not work for you, and you cannot ask him to do anything." Well, my father knew this deacon of the church that approached his son, and he said to my dad, "quoting" well, George, "I saw him standing there, and I didn't think you would mind." Well, my father said to the young deacon that I am only to be addressed as Rev. Galloway. The white guy then said in return to my father that they call our minister Dan, and he didn't have a problem with that. And my father told the young deacon again, "You are to only address me as Reverend or Pastor Galloway." George stood there in disbelief as to how our dad told that white man and wasn't afraid to let him know what he stood for. As they continued to load the car, the deacon stood to the side and addressed my father saying, "Good day to you, Reverend Galloway." My father said, "And you as well."

When my dad got into the car, he told my brother that "You are never to let no one disrespect you and address you in a way that is unacceptable to your title." By the end of the first complete school year, they attended the school with no other problem. Barbara got the leading role for the *Wizard of Oz*, and my parents were so proud of her. She also received honor ribbons at the school ceremony. My parents were so proud of their kids for just being the bravest young kids considering the circumstances they had to endure but with the determination of my father to accept no for an answer and not letting fear get in the way they learned that anything is possible if you stay focus and fight till the very end to win the outcome of the victory. My siblings integrated that school in Selma, Alabama, and made a statement and made it possible so that I and my younger siblings and many other black children could attend any school of our choice. And my father faced the white school board alone and prepared his children to be treated and given the same opportunity as the white kids was his ultimate goal, and he succeeded. The next school year, he enrolled the fourth child with no problem. President Johnson signed the end to segregation in 1964. My father knew that one day black history would make its mark and be told and placed in all schools so that all children would share together in a classroom no matter their race of what his children made possible for many and that one day they would be as proud as he and my mother was. My father always told my siblings to believe in themselves, take a stand, make a difference, and know your worth, and you will accomplish your goals and dreams.

Chapter 4
The Truth Marches On

The family was growing each year, now with another daughter Mary born into the heart of the movement. My father still insisted that the kids remained at Baker School, and they were doing well, and achievements were being met even if the white folks didn't approve there was not much they could do about it, and the fight was still as real as ever in Selma. Mass meetings were as strong as ever at Browns Chapel and even though that summer of 1964 Judge James Hare issued an injunction making it illegal for three or more people to congregate. This made the demonstrations and voter registration work almost impossible while the SNCC pursued the slow appeals process. Although the Justice Department was pursuing its own legal action to address discrimination against black voters, their attorneys offered no protection and did nothing to intervene when Sherriff Clark and local officials openly flaunted the 1957 Civil Rights Acts. With no help from the FBI, they refused to protect the civil rights workers. They would watch an attack and did nothing. My father would get very frustrated when he would take some of his church members to register, and more than 350 African Americans would stand in line all day, and the registrar would only process forty applications, and white lawmen refused to allow people to leave the line and return after spending the entire day trying to get blacks registered. My father later that evening met with the other eight leaders, and they had a meeting, and they all agreed that Reverend Reese would write a letter inviting Dr. Martin Luther King and the SCLC to come to Selma to lend their support to the voting rights campaign. King and SCLC agreed to come. My father got with his security detail group to set up security knowing that Martin Luther King was coming. He knew that he would have to have in place a security detail route to keep him safe. On the day of King's arrival, they started their support to the voting rights campaign on January 2, 1965, with a meeting in violation of an injunction against large gatherings. My father was there from the beginning. The fight was real, and it was on the final stage by the time King's arrival. He and many other ministers and teachers really had a breaking point on January 22, 1965. When Mrs. Boynton was physically attacked, they took a stand. Ministers and teachers marched right to the courthouse to protest knowing that there was an injunction for them not to gather in large groups to protest, but they had taken many stands and knew what the consequences were. They had been down that road many a times, but they knew they needed to make a stand. They were not arrested, but they were told to move away from in front of the courthouse. They were not afraid. My father stood there with many others until their point was made. The morning of February 1 started off as usual, my father getting ready to go to Browns Chapel for a morning meeting. When he arrived at the church, Rev. Martin L. King and others decided that on that day, they would march down to the courthouse. When they approached the courthouse, they were arrested. My father was jailed with Martin Luther King and others for eight days. They prayed and sang and prayed, and in between the prayers, they were served black-eyed peas. They were served black-eyed peas twice a day. My father remembered they had no taste and wasn't given the choice of salt and pepper. The taste was very bland. After all, they were in Sheriff Clark's jail, so he definitely wanted the stay to be as miserable as possible. They were only given water once a day, and some of the men that were locked up needed to take medications but were not able to because when they were arrested. They were not allowed to contact their loved ones to bring their meds to them.

On the ninth day, my father was released alone with the other men. My father went home, and my mother knew he was in jail because her aunt Hester went to the jail looking for her daughter Bessie and was told that she was arrested with him. My father cleaned up and ate a much-needed hot meal, and the security workers came to the house for a meeting. My mother at this time was pregnant with me and was due to have me in March. Trying not to worry and take care of the other six children was a full-time job, so she just prayed that God would keep him out of harm's way and left the rest in God's hands. My father, with a couple of his members, went to Marion on February 18 for a night march. Marion Alabama always came to Selma to protest and march, and Selma knew of the march, so my father and others went. My father remembered at the church where they gathered before they started to march they had a service and then proceeded to march, and all of a sudden, they were ambushed and attacked. They started to run. Screams and cries filled the streets. My father made way around the back of the church, and it was dark. The law officers had broken out the streetlights. They cried out for help. With all the screaming and people panicking and running, there was no telling what type of injuries people were enduring. His aide and the other deacons made it to my father's car, and they left Marion praying to make it out safe. By the time they made it back to Selma, word was out that a white state trooper shot a young black man by the name of Jimmie Lee Jackson. The next day, they called for a mass meeting, and my father went to Browns Chapel, where James Bevel spoke at a rally calling for a march to Montgomery to the state capitol. The anger that came over the freedom fighters took an even bigger stand to get a message across. My father with others and his aide, Ms. Lilly, loaded up a couple of caskets and drove to Montgomery and placed the caskets on the capitol and protest to Gov. Wallace that black lives matter and wanted a change to end police brutality. Of course, the governor did not take a liking to the caskets being left on the capitol's steps, but by the time the authorities were notified about the caskets being there on the capitol steps, my father and the other that were with him had left the caskets and were back in Selma, and my father never spoke a word to anyone about what they had done. He made it back home, pulled himself together, prayed, studied the Word, and went to Jimmie Lee Jackson's funeral. Later that morning, as he drove up to Browns Chapel with many people already standing outside the church, he drove past the front of the church and proceeded to park. There was a sign place on the church stating, "Racism killed our brother," and they were also listening to Rev. Martin L. King saying Jackson was murdered by the brutality of every sheriff who practiced lawlessness in the name of law.

The feeling and the mood in that church on that day had my father feeling like the fight must go on because this could easily have been his son. Things have to change. No one should ever have to lose their life fighting for their freedom. Later that week, on Sunday, at my father's church, he spoke to his congregation, letting them know that the DCLV Dallas County Voter League, a group that he was a part of, and the local activists were pushing for the march to Montgomery. As he was speaking to his congregation that morning, he had this pull of fiery courage and strength with no fear, and as he continued to speak to his congregation, he said, "We must not sit by and let the lawmen do as they please and take the lives of our inno-cent black youths and adults. We must take a stand." My father went on to tell them that next week on Sunday, they would be marching to Montgomery. Yes, as we all know, this was the day that marchers were assaulted, and this day was called Bloody Sunday. The people started talking about the march from Selma to Montgomery. A couple of days before the march, one of the white families whose kid received piano lessons from my dad informed my father that the local officers were mentioning using tear gas to deter the march. My father took this information to Reverend Anderson and told him that at the next mass meeting, they had one of a servicemen who trained in chemical warfare in the army to give a crash course on how to react to tear gas. As the training session was happening, my father thought about when he was in the army and was in training in the gas chamber as part of their preparation for war. Never would he have ever thought that his encounter would be on the streets of Selma, Alabama, fight-ing for my rights. My father, mother, and her grandmother were so deeply saddened with what happened in Marion that they all made the decision to join the march as well. My mother being in her ninth month of pregnancy with me felt that she needed to be there. On the morning of the march, the family had a prayer, ate breakfast, and started out as if it was going to be finally the prayer of protesting and standing up, that being jailed was finally going to not be in vain, and they were going to march to Montgomery and make a stand. My father was getting ready to head over to Browns Chapel, and he told my mother and my grandmother to head down to Rexall Drugstore, and they could watch the march from there. When my father arrived at Browns Chapel, the lineup was being arranged. Dr. King was not at the church. He was not going to march with us due to other engagements. As we proceeded down Sylvan Street and turned onto Broad Street, hands joined together walking four people in each line over Edmond Pettus Bridge, and at the bottom of the bridge were state troopers on horses and troopers on feet in a line with protector shields. Standing beside them was Sheriff Clarke and his deputy with billy club in hand. My father's first thought went straight into prayer mode, talking to God and saying, "Build a fence around us all, Holy Spirit," taking his fresh iron handkerchief from his back pocket and wiping his forehead even though it was not warm sweat beaded on his forehead. My father was located about the ninth row, and as they stopped marching, he heard coming from the bottom of the bridge an officer demanding for them to go back. The officer took the speaker and told them he didn't care where they would go, they just could not stay on this bridge, and there would not be a march today.

As the SCLC leader proceeded to ask if he could speak, everything went into chaos. All of a sudden, my father was grasping for breath. The tear gas had overcome him. He staggered out of the smoke, and he heard horses galloping behind him. As he moved more closer to the left side of the bridge and moved quickly backward toward downtown on the same side his family would be standing on, he prayed that his family had left in time before the troopers on horses would make it to downtown as he was looking around Ms. Lilly had followed his same steps behind him and was running beside him, screaming Oh my God. He remember seeing Ms. Lilly raising her hand up with the trooper striking her, and she put her hand up to block the stick. My father remembered his eyes burning and running, half blinded by the smoke. People were falling, being beaten, tripping on top of one another. He never got struck. He saw children running. As he made his way to Rexall Drugstore and didn't his see family and not knowing if they were safe, he proceeded to go home. When he got to the house, my mom and the rest of the family made it home safely, running for their lives. By the grace of God, no one was hurt. They were more frightened to death than anything else. My father left the house. After seeing that everyone was fine, he headed to Browns Chapel. When he got there, it looked like a makeshift hospital after a war. Ms. Lilly walked up to my father and asked if his family was safe. As she was holding her hand, she had a twisted thumb and was bruised as if she had taken a bad fall. People were walking around in disbelief. Others were coming out of G. W. Carvers homes, fleeing from the troopers who chased them all the way back to Browns Chapel. The police officers were now driving and on horses, passing by the church. So much tension was in the air. There were a lot of my father's church members that had cuts and bruises. My father saw Sis. Minnie Strugg, a nurse who would later become my godmother, was asked by my father if any of the injured people she was treating needed a ride to the hospital. Many people were using their own car to take people who were badly injured to the hospital. Sister Strugg then told my father that a prayer would be something we all could use at this time. He did just that; he started off his prayer, asking God to heal and "Make the souls out here today fine in body physically, and we all accept the Spirit of our heavenly Father to dwell with us all and have control through Christ Jesus. Amen." With the tension in the air, my father who was the head of security at Browns Chapel immediately stepped up the security details for overnight watch, making sure the church did not get bombed there. Word got out that a lot of the white locals were threatening to burn down the church, so no more meetings could take place. My father met with his security details that night to communicate the scheduling. He set up a tight schedule with two men in the front and two covering the back of the church. They also discussed with others leaders that some of the groups wanted to march again right away, but Martin Luther King didn't think the timing was right. However, with everyone's tensions so high, and this town was used to the push back from the authorities and the attacks they had been in this freedom fight for some time now, and they were not going to just give up and give in and let the whites win. They would not let them scare them into quitting, so the agreement was set for March 9. They would march again to Montgomery, and this time, Martin Luther King was going to join them.

Rev. Galloway, and other leaders, in the civil rights movement, preform a March, and all were arrested.

He told all the organizers in that meeting that he was going to issue a call for people to come to Selma and support the effort, and with my father being over the Selma's visitors, he received a lot of calls from white clergyman saying that they would travel to Selma and attend the march. My father went home pretty late that night because he stayed and worked a late shift till around 2:00 a.m.

Curfew was set in place in Selma; no one was allowed to be out after ten o'clock in the evening, so he carefully drove home praying the entire way, but he felt that God was there with him, always guiding and protecting. As he was driving home, he saw police activity heavy that night more than usual. It was almost as if the bloody Sunday gave the white lawmen the more power to mistreat blacks even more. Elements of the 82nd Airborne were brought to Selma for about two weeks. The United States Army took over traffic control in Selma. They were under martial law. Selma was literally under siege. Many of the soldiers were black. The Alabama National Guard was federalized and had to protect them. On March 9, the family was up early. Kids were getting ready for school, and my father was getting ready for the march. He told the kids that the march would happen that day and they had lots of visitors and Reverend King would march as well. The day of this march, my father said there were people from all walks of life who came from many cities to Selma to take a stand. Selma had visitors from all over; and my father, being over the visitors, logged in priests, nuns, bishops, and ministers from many states. Browns Chapel was filled with many supporters, and this morning, they were getting the line up as to where everyone will be placed for the march to Montgomery. They started the day off with a prayer, and my father led them with a selective song on the piano. Rev. Martin L. King said a speech, and they proceeded to start the walk from Browns Chapel. It was the most beautiful sight the eye could see. The crowd that consist of children, older folks, young folks, whites and blacks joined together singing negro spirituals as they approached the bridge. As they approached the bridge and topped the bridge, the paste of walking came to a stop, and with my father being on the right side and about the six rows back on the end, a calmness came over him as if God was saying, "Peace, be still." The people in front started to kneel, so he kneeled, and the ministers beside him kneeled as well. As the crowd started to rise back up, Rev. Martin. L King started to head back down the hill toward the church. The organizers met with Reverend King. They discussed him turning around, and my father remembered having a conversation with Reverend Anderson about God speaking on that bridge to him as well, and turning around was the right thing to do. This day was known as Turn Around Tuesday. After they finished the meeting, my father went home and took my older siblings Barbara and George to the warehouse where all the supplies were being stocked, and the rest of his crew met them at the warehouse. My father had all the inventory logged and accounted for. They loaded cars and took much-needed supplies to homes of the needy and the poor.

With many spectators who came to town for the march, a lot of the churches brought busloads and carloads of blankets, clothes, and food to Brown Chapel as fast as my father could unload. He and my brother and sister, with help of the crew, were packing cars and taking supplies back to the warehouse to separate and place items on the inventory the list. On Sunday, March 14, my father preached on courage at his church. He said, "These true men of God suffered for the sake of Jesus and his Gospel and also the faith they had in Jesus and his Father, our *eternal everlasting* God and Father. Therefore, understand the everlasting God and Father. Therefore, I understand the evil forces that are at work in the United States of America, a country that seems to have no soul. However, *please*, you and I must not despair nor faint. You all men and women must hold sound doctrine, and we must suffer as Christ did to prove that the God we talk about is able to *free us.*" He then went on to tell his congregation that "We all are intelligent and have many gifts given to us by God our father to use and the world can't take these gifts away from us. We are to use our gifts to the highest degree. And if you are saying "how" Some people believe there is nothing one man can or woman can do against the enormous array of this world's fills. Yet many of the world's greatest movements of thought and actions have flowed from the work of a single man like Rev. Martin Luther King. A young monk began the Protestant Reformation. A young general extended an empire form Macedonia to the borders of the earth. A young woman reclaimed the territory of France. It was a young Italian who explored and discovered the new world and the thirty-two-year-old Thomas Jefferson who explained that all men are created equal. These men moved the world, and so can we. Few will have the greatness to bend history itself, but each of us can work to change a small portion of events, and in total of all those acts will be written the history of this sad generation. Each time we stand for ideals or acts to improve the lot of others or strike out against injustice, we send fourth a tiny ripple of hope and crossing each other from a million different centers of energy and daring, those ripples to build a current that can swap down the mightiest walls of oppression and resistance, and I believe that those in this generation with the courage to enter the moral conflict will find themselves with companions in every corner of the globe. There is hope. You and God are the majority, and God can't lose. Just let man see Jesus in you. Faith can't lose. It's on the streets of America, in the school of the so-called learning, in God's house of worship, in the courts of America, in the state government, and all the homes of America especially the white homes. But we must forgive try to love the unlovable with a sweet attitude so that God's wrath will not come upon us." He then closed off his sermon with the song "Lift Every Voice And Sing." My father felt that day that he had received this message from God and needed for many that was at church on that day to know that we cannot give up. The enemy is weaker than the mighty, and nothing is going to stop us or turn us around, and as long as we hold onto God's unchanging hand, the Lord God Almighty will always build a fence around his believers who don't waiver. The conversation that he had with the deacon board members that day after church services asking if any of them would be available to give some time to help with the security at Browns Chapel due to what happened on Bloody Sunday, and they were shorthanded. He got a lot of volunteers who would help. This day felt like he had accomplished a lot. The next day, my father met with the young folks at Brown Chapel. They were still protesting and planning sit-ins. As he worked with the civil rights choir and some of the youth freedom fighters, beside him stood his own son, young but interested at heart and passionate about the movement. He spoke to them, saying, "I will keep encouraging you all. You all are so very young and have much to do for God and his people of not only in Selma, and to remember the basic value, the one thing that really matters is to be bigger than the things that can happen to you. Nothing that can happen to you is half as important as the way in which you meet it. I have realized that here is the basic of the only real security and peace of mind that man can have. Nobody can be sure when disaster, disappointments, injustice, or humiliation may come to you through no fault of one's own. Nor can we be guaranteed against our own mistakes and failures, but the way we meet life is ours to choose and integrity, fortitude, dignity, and compassion are our choices. The things that can happen to us lose their power over us. Let not your hearts be troubled, nor let it be afraid." That same evening, it rained very heavily, and my father had taken a lot of the students to go door-to-door handing out forms and encouraging blacks on the east side where Craig Airforce Base was open and operating at the time to vote.

My father was told by one of the other organizers that the east side was flooding and that a lot of the students that they had in the field were in danger due to the rising floodwaters. My father got in his car drove over the Edmond Pettus Bridge and retrieved those students. They were cold and wet from the floodwaters but still determined. These young people were the heart and soul of this movement, and they wanted and needed their freedom of speech and the right to vote not only for their parents and themselves but for the future generation. A lot of these students were attending Hudson High, and it was very easy for them to understand what the fight was about because they had parents who needed their help to pass the literacy test and comprehension of the constitution. The black population in Selma in 1965 was 57 percent, but of the 15,000 blacks old enough to vote, only 130 were registered (fewer than 1 percent). At one time, more than 80 percent of Dallas County blacks lived below the poverty line—most of them working as sharecroppers, farm, hands, maids, janitors, and day laborers. So most of these young freedom fighters knew the situation their parents were in, and most of them were either afraid to take a stand because their jobs and home could be in jeopardy of being taken away. There have been 950 students absent from Hudson High on some days of these marches. They were sent to different prisons, and a lot of the parents had no idea where their children were until my father and other leaders would inform them of where their children were being detained.

These young freedom fighters endured being attacked by two hundred or more deputies. Some of whom were KKK. They were armed with electric cattle prods, and these students were whipped as they ran on foot and being chased by men on horses, carrying long leather whips, and beaten with clubs. These students took this treatment all for the sake of their rights. Not for something that they were taking that didn't belong to them but as a country, tis of thee the sweet land of one's liberty, this United States of America. Their family fought and died for this country. They did not deserve to be treated as second-class citizens. These students are willing to lay down their lives for this movement, and it touched my dad to the core to see the young folks so passionate about the movement. On March 15, the movement was still in full swing, and many folks from out of town stayed to see this through till the end. Some of the white northerners stayed with many black families. President Lyndon Johnson went on national television to pledge his support to the Selma protestor and called for the passage of a new voting rights bill that he was introducing to Congress. My mother still pregnant with me and due any day, and Father sat watching, listening to the president say, "There is no negro problem, there is no Southern problem, there is no Northern problem, and there is only an America problem." He then continued to speak, saying, "Their cause must be our cause too." My parents were sitting, continuing to listen to the president's speech. The telephone rang, and my father answered, and it was one of the organizing members telling him that a meeting had been put together at Browns Chapel pertaining to the president's speech. By the time my father came back to the living room to finish watching the speech, the president was saying that "All of us must overcome the crippling legacy of bigotry and injustice. And We *shall* overcome." My father just stood there for a moment and then told my mother that they called for a meeting at Browns Chapel and that since they were on baby watch, he shouldn't be gone too long. He arrived at Browns Chapel, went inside where all of the leaders of all the group were coming in as well. The discussion was mainly about them going to get demonstration approve for the march. The next day, March 16, Selma demonstrators submitted a detailed march plan to federal Judge M. Johnson, who approved the demonstrators and enjoined Governor Wallace and law enforcement from harassing or threatening marchers. When the news spread over Selma that they were going to be allowed to march, my father received two telephone calls from two of the white families telling him if he continued to participate in the marches that his service would no longer be needed. So, of course, my father said that we all have to do what we have to do and standing up for his rights were a priority and he could not let his people down or his family and their future.

On March 17, President Johnson submitted voting rights legislation to Congress. Now it was a waiting game. That did not stop my dad from continuing to take some of his congregation to try and get them registered. He told his son George that the fight must go on even though they were turned away with the same excuse that stating that the registration office was closed my father still went every day all the way up until March 20, the day President Johnson federalized the Alabama National Guard to oversee the Selma to Montgomery march. My father headed down to the church for the meeting with the other leaders he took Barbara and George with him to Browns Chapel. They started preparing the security detail and how the crowd would be handled and how Martin Luther King would be on the front line with a list of marchers that was given out to keep control of the protest line and the safety. They also discussed the reducing of the size of the crowd to only three hundred chosen to march the entire trip, and my father and his security details were among the three hundred who will complete the entire march from Selma to Montgomery. The plan was very detailed about the campsites as to where they were located and how on the last leg of the march leading up to the complex of St. Jude where there would be a big concert. This was the last campsite, and this was where the three hundred marchers would receive bright-orange vests. They were called the nucleus marchers. They would be set apart walking in the forefront, leading the march from the Catholic hospital school church complex of St. Jude to the platform set before the marble steps at the capitol. They closed out the late night, and he walked in the house, and my mother up baked Bernice's birthday cake for the day after. He told my mom that he wasn't going to be here for her birthday cake cutting after she would get out of school because they would leave for the Montgomery march by then. My mother already knew because it was all over town that everyone would be participating in the march tomorrow. Even the kids knew about the big march. It's all everyone was talking about. My mother had already put together a knapsack with a change of clean shirts and extra things he may need on the trip earlier that evening. My father was just praying and hoping that the baby wouldn't arrive while he was marching to Montgomery.

Chapter 5
Fifty Miles to Freedom

March 21, 1965, was the day of the march from Selma to Montgomery. My father went into the kitchen, and the children were eating breakfast, and George asked if he could go with him to the march. He answered no, because someone needed to take care of the women and make sure Mom is taken care of in case she goes into labor. He then wished Bernice a happy birthday. For some reason, George already knew he wasn't going to church or the march, because no clothes were ironed for him to put on for church. He was really upset and wanted to go. He was so used to going everywhere with our father. He surely wish he could go. My dad told George that "One day, you will understand why this fight for us as a threat to the basic law of the Constitution was most clearly evident, where the battle for human rights was most clearly slated and drawn. And when I was in the army serving during World War II, soldiers went all over the world not we trust to interfere in the internal affairs of other nations but to defend the principle of liberty for all people everywhere. We the marchers have produced the great movement of numbers of Negros together and for the first time giving a whole body of men the courage and the solidarity to resist intimidation and tyranny effectively and consistently." My father went on to say as the kids listened to him that "This day is very important not only for you and your siblings but their children and the future generations." Mother continued fixing packed lunches for him to make the trip and placed the sandwiches in a brown paper bag. My dad thought, "Since I'm going to be in the outdoor elements, I better pack the rubbing alcohol as well." Grandmother Mary was helping the kids get ready because they was going to watch the march from Broad Street. Not wanting to miss history herself, she hurried everyone along so they could head downtown. My father headed for the door, said his goodbyes, and grabbed his long trench coat and hat. The weather man called for rain for the next three days, so he placed the rubber shoe covers over his Dexter soft-bottom ankle boots to keep his foots from getting totally soaked. It was a cold overcast day, in the midtwenties. My father headed to the church. When he drove up at Browns Chapel, it was a sea of people all in the streets. Every news station from as far as the Northern states to the bottom of the South Florida Pan handle were there. The church service at Brown Chapel was filled with the spirits high among high, and you could fill the spirit of emotions mixed with defeat all over that church inside and out. My father played the piano that morning for the church service on that glorious day of history taking place. Martin Luther King spoke outside on the top steps of the church. This was truly a day to remember for not only Selma Alabama but for the entire world. They placed lei bouquet around Martin Luther King neck and many of the leaders form the SCLC, DCVL, and the SNCC. The cold overcast day as they started out was not noticeably because it was so much excitement in the air till you didn't even notice the cold. As they start out for the street, the lines formed, and they started the journey from Selma to Montgomery. My father's security team and the SCLC security team formed a hand link chain on both sides of the march with Martin Luther King and many other leaders in the inside walking down the street until the crowd somewhat thinned out, giving a wider line of walking room for the leader. My father was on the right side of the march about the sixth row back on the outside, and as they approached Sylvan Street and Alabama Avenue, my mother called out my father's name when she saw him marching and took this picture of him heading toward the Edmond Pettus Bridge. He recalled looking back as far as the eye could see. There were people from all over the world who joined this marched, walking side by side, hands joined—blacks and whites together. In his powerful speech, Martin Luther King asked the people to "Come and walk with us. Join us." People came by the thousands. The reporters stated that there were twenty-five thousand people gathered. George Wallace sent his troops closer into Selma. As they continued to march, the troops were informed to let the leaders know that some would have to turn around. The leaders and security details were well aware that the troop detail was only set up to be able to protect three hundred marchers. Once all the marchers got past the Edmond Pettus Bridge, they turned all but three hundred around right where the highway narrows from four lanes to two lanes. The number reduced to three hundred marchers. The National Guard was notified by the organizers as to where the line stopped at and stood guard to control the count of the chosen ones who could continue the entire walk to Montgomery.

They walked till midmorning. The number had grown out to about 450, and just before noon, he stopped for lunch of tuna fish sandwiches and cold chocolate drinks. My father and other leaders were forced to thin ranks, not allowing the extra to continue on with the march with them. It started out cold, but as they continued to walk, it warmed up, and my father took his coat off and tied the arms of the coat around his neck as so many other men on that line did. Now don't think for one minute that were having a peaceful walk. The KKK walked on the other side of the street throwing out notes wrapped around a rock with threatening gestures written on the paper. One of the young ladies who was walking on the line picked up the rock and started to read it out loud. The note said, "Deer M. L. Koon," spelled in that fashion, which tells you that they were ignorant and with no sense on how to even know how to write a proper note. The note said that "You all will never make it to Montgomery." Another note read, "We have bombs planted all along the way, and we got helicopter that's going to drop poison gas on you." A lot of the notes that the younger freedom fighters were reading told us to turn our nappy-headed selves around and get off our highway. Now my father was thinking as the young marchers were reading these notes that they can barely spell, and most of them haven't even went and fought for their country but had the nerve to say it's their highway, but my father was not going to let those white folks scare him into turning around. He didn't care; he was determined. He had to walk. He had to finish. "We all here walking and had to knock down degradation, segregation, immorality that stood in our way." My father was willing to put his life on the line to make sure the future of his children and the rest of the black generation have a voice and a choice. The National Guard was present along the march with water tanks. They stopped in the late evening as dark fell. They walked about seven miles. The first night stop was in a cornfield where tents had been pitched, and it was where my father was served their first meal. Drinking water was provided. It was carried in a tank truck and was heavy with the taste of chemicals used for purification. The nurses who were located at the first campsite told them about a remedy to be able to within stand the taste of the water. She instructed them to pop a Alka-Seltzer tablet in their water, and this would fizz away the bad taste. The nurses at this first campsite were placed here to treat only blisters and sunburn. My father recalled sitting and look-ing over the fields, listening to the National Guard helicopters flying overhead and thinking, "This is all for my children so that one day they will have the freedom and the right to vote and be anything in this world they wanted to be. Then he started praying, asking God to cover the family back in Selma and hoping that my mother wouldn't go into labor while he was on this journey. He was thinking that the five-day trip is worth it for standing up and believing and never giving up. This long-awaited freedom march was well overdue. As he was sitting, the larger crowd started singing freedom songs, so he got up and went over to join them. He talked to some of the white priests and ministers and young freedom fighters and listened to them talk about their experience and what all this meant to them. Tired from the first haul with aching feet, he dismissed himself and went over to where he was assigned to sleep, took out his alcohol and rubbed it on his weary feet, lay down on his sleepy bag in the tent that was set up for the leaders, and went to sleep.

On Monday morning, March 22, day 2 of the march, my father looked over the field, and the morning dew was like snow on the ground. It reminded him of when he lived in Virginia and the ground was covered from the snowfall in the middle of the night and would wake to a snow-covered ground the next morning. The ground was cold and wet from the rain, but the sleeping bag and blanket stood the test and kept him pretty warm and dry. He ate the breakfast that was prepared, and they started the second day of the march. There were men of a special bomb disposal unit who wore bright red baseball hats who scouted ahead of the marchers, checking under every culvert and bridge. "We will probably find nothing," said one of the officers, "but it's a precaution we have to take to keep everyone safe." The other precautions included a tricky traffic shuffle, with troopers blocking traffic about a mile ahead and a mile behind us, and they sent the traffic through one line at a time on a schedule coordinated by radio. My father and other leaders were given the information of what the route security points would be, and they helped keep the line of marchers close together. Traffic moved over the road with only minor delays, and the reduced contingent of marchers swung along briskly, covering about two miles an hour, with a ten-minute break every hour. They walked and sang freedom songs and walked and sang between the ten-minute breaks. They stumbled with swollen feet and ankles. They didn't care. They were determined. By noon, the feeding consisted of sandwiches and chocolate drink, and they sat in the field eating with the temperature now feeling like seventy. The journey was real, and the fight was real fight for freedom. By nightfall on Monday, more than three thousand troops were assigned to the detail about ten for each marcher. They came to the next overnight campsite. They marched for about seventeen miles that day. It rained on them that evening, but they kept right on marching. Wearing that hat helped because it at least kept his head covered. Dr. King held an impromptu press conference on the tailgate of a panel truck, and a sign of how tired a lot of the marchers had become, they really didn't crowd around as they usually did wherever and whenever he spoke. Most of them instead lay on the damp hard ground with their plate of beans and tomatoes, saying little until the evening songfest and speeches began. King ended his speech, saying the march would cover nine or ten miles on the day after enough to get the marchers back on the double-barreled miles on stretch of highway—another sixteen on Wednesday and the final three on Thursday. Many of them including my father turned in almost immediately, curling up in sleeping bags, blankets in tents that were set up. Tuesday, Morning

March 23, day 3 was cold damp, but they were well rested, eating breakfast with his head and shoulders draped in a blanket to protect him from the early morning cold all geared up to march this ten-mile stretch. As they marched all day singing and the younger student's horse playing around full of energy, they marched through the swamp land and rolling Alabama hills. The hills looked like mountains as they climbed them with nothing but pastures and fields up ahead. They were tired and weary but determined and continued walking. They had lunch served on the side of the road in the fields and then continued on like an army in battle. The temperature was in the midseventies. As they sat taking a break, Andrew Young, Rev. Martin Luther King's aide, dressed in overalls and huddled over a group of young high schoolboys and gave them a lesson in the economics of the area. He told the young boys that the whites want to drive us out of here. They don't need us anymore. They needed us only to plant and harvest the cotton. But now they put their fields of cotton, peanuts, and corn into the soil bank and get paid by the government. They don't need us, and they want to keep the political balance. It doesn't matter how they keep this political balance by either driving us out or by killing us. But they won't do this, because we outbreed them."

The March from Selma to Montgomery, Rev. Galloway is ready for the 50 mile foot March

My father sat there listening and thinking, "What a great point, and it is something our young folks need to stay focus on." They completed the ten miles and got to the third campsite. The water was a bit better at Trickum; and a planned supper of baked bean, sliced tomatoes, canned fruit, and cookie was waiting. There was always a speaker every night with music entertainment to keep the mood up, and the campsites in supporters' yards made it much safer, and a lot of the marchers felt at ease. Calling it a night after the entertainment was finished and getting some rest was on the minds of the majority, except for the young folks. They talked and sang till late before they finally calmed down. The morning of March 24, Wednesday, day 4, started out cloudy with no sun. They finished breakfast, and the marchers started out singing freedom songs and marching as they started the sixteen-mile march. The dark clouds moved in, and it started to rain. They laughed at the rain. They took off their shoes, and they splashed through the puddles. They sang their spiritual songs louder and better than ever before. The rain did not dampen anyone's spirits. My father's coat was soaked, but he felt that he couldn't have it any other way, because the way he saw it, this was for the movement. My father though, "After all, if we're going to tell our grandchildren about this march, we have to have a few tales of hardship so that many will know what they sacrifice." Nuns picked up the bottom of their robes, and marched on yelling out, "It feels like we have ten pounds of water at the bottom of our robes." The young black boys made their own hats to shelter from rain. One wore a cornflake box. Others wrapped large pieces of plastic sheet around them and over their heads. But it rain so hard that the black dye from the one of the priest's hat trickled down his neck. My father was thinking, "Thank God for the rain," and covered up, but with the amount of rain that was coming down, it felt like the shoes had five pounds of water in them. The scenery changed a bit on Wednesday, the fourth day of the march, because at the stopping point at lunchtime, many of them took off soaking shoes and were rubbing their feet because they all had blisters from walking with their feet being soaked in their shoes from the rain. My father took off his boots and soothed his aching feet in roadside stream during milk-and-sandwich break on highway to Montgomery. As they started back on the march, the rain came off, and on they walked through the big swamp and over rolling hills where brown and white cows and black angus cattle peered over barbed wire fences staring at them. They were singing Harry Belafonte songs. The young folks got a big enjoyment with those songs. Then as they approached the city, there were billboards and hotdog stands and a gas station. They had marched only a short distance along the two-lane highway when they came to the four-lane divided strip of US-80 highway, leading on toward Montgomery. Thereafter, bus after bus brought additional marchers to join them. By nine o'clock, there were close to seven hundred. By the time they filed into the campsite at three, there were three thousand. Businesses along the highway leading into Montgomery were closed for the most part. And the long private roads leading to farms there were newly painted "No Trespassing Signs." Dr. King, who was in Cleveland overnight for a speaking engagement, joined the marchers at the airport, which was about five miles from the campsite.

Just as the group was entering Montgomery over the bridge, the sky opened up again for more than fifteen minutes. Pouring rain and high winds. The rain and the wind knocked down a huge tent at St. Jude's campsite under which the show was to be held. Bu the marchers were not in low spirits. They kept right on, singing and making up songs about the Wallace all in fun. Reverend King led the singing America and the "Battle Hymn" by the students along the road from George Wallace Carver School. My father was singing his heart out despite the blisters on his feet for the past two days and picked up his pace as they entered into the camp. They camped on Wednesday outside the downtown section of Montgomery on the grounds of St. Jude's Catholic Hospital, and those who marched the fifty miles and those who joined the marchers for the final leg of the journey were entertained at outdoor show. The talent included Sammy Davis Jr, who closed his New York show to come down there for the night; Harry Belafonte, comedian Dick Gregory, Bobby Darin, Tony Bennett, Chad Mitchell Trio, folksinger Odetta, Nina Simone, Billy Eckstine, and Alan King. Some fifteen thousand people packed the football field at St. Jude's for the show. Equipment was late in arriving, and the marchers stood around for nearly two hours waiting for the concert to start. Some of the women collapsed due to just exhaustion in itself and were taken to the hospital. My father and a couple of the other men put together crates to make a stage since the storm had destroyed the setup. Reverend Anderson told one of the entertainers, "If your piano player doesn't make it to the show, then we have a very good piano player that can fill in," and he pointed at my father. Sammy Davis Jr. said, "I just might have to take him up on that offer." My father met up with Pastor Nicholson and some of his church members who came by car to the campsite, and my father asked how the family was doing. He told my father that there was no baby news and that Minnie Strugg stopped by to check on her every day and his wife as well. He felt relieved. There were food and drinks served, with plenty of excitement and great entertainment. There was singing and joyful laughter, with the stars shining bright after the storm had passed over that day, and the evening was closed out with a joining song of "I Am Not Goanna Let Nobody Turn Me Around." What a powerful way to end the night. Thursday, March 25, the fifth and final day of the march, the camp site was buzzing with excitement. Everyone was up. They served breakfast, and they got the lineup, ready to head to the capitol for the rally and Dr. King's speech. Skies were gray and rainy and spotted, and helicopters hovering above. As my father was talking with Reverend Abernathy and Reverend Anderson, one of the other leaders interrupted, stating that a Montgomery Deputy was talking to Dr. King and others. He was delivering a message from Judge L. S. Moore of Dallas County, serving an injunction and summons and ordering the carpooling to bring civil rights leaders from Selma to Montgomery. The SCLC and the SNCC were served noticed of a suit of $1 million, which was filed by the city of Selma, and for 9,750 by the local bus company.

The complaints seek damages for a bus boycott and operation of the carpool along routes exclusively franchised by the bus firm. Reverend Abernathy said to the deputy, "We are not trying to put anyone out of business. We are trying to put freedom into business." The deputy handed the papers to him and walked away. My father and the other two ministers who were standing there were not going to let Selma win. We are the *winners* on this day," my father said. As they looked at the ranks of marchers, it swelled from twenty thousand to thirty thousand. As they lined up, the three hundred nucleus marchers set apart by the privilege of wearing brilliant-orange vests from the Catholic hospital school church complex of St. Jude to the platform set before the marble capitol steps they walked in the forefront. They were in line which moved six across the broad athletic fields of St. Jude. My father was next to Reverend Sherill, a clergymen from Ipswich. One of the ministers who made the entire march was talking to Andrew Young about how he was so moved with the strength and fight the young freedom fighters were about the movement and that he would like to take a couple of students back to Ipswich Mass to start up a voting rally and give them an outlook of outside of Selma. Andrew Young told Reverend Sherill, "Why don't you take back a busload?" My father said, "They are fighters for their rights. I worked with many of them. They are serious when it comes to the movement on fair and equal justice and standing up for your rights and sticking with it until the end." So the three of them agreed to work on making that happen. As they marched, they held up signs that said, "God Is Color Blind," "Closed for Freedom Day," "I'll Be Marching with You." My father was thinking as he walked through the streets of Montgomery in the front line that "This is the message pounded in the mud by military boots and by the fragile shoes of white nuns, and priests and white ministers, and it was pounded into the pavement by the sneakers and by the bare feet of the freedom fighter students and the entertainers that came to entertain and then decided to join the march. Somehow this message came to the young that watched and waved as we marched to the end, so it could be the beginning of their future. On this day, history came to the sound of song and the tread of feet, and arm in arm, blacks and whites marched while waving and screaming, 'Freedom," and thank you, for this was the march for their tomorrow." America was treading on the soul of Alabama, and never again would Alabama be the same. They stood as their arms locked and their hands clasped, and their voices and bodies crossed the grand plaza as they sang "We Shall Overcome." Once they all made it to the capitol, Reverend King gave a powerful speech no one who witnessed this history-making day will ever forget. Once they started to leave the capitol, the mood in the air was unbelievable. They loaded up the cars they had set up for all the leaders and followed the buses out of Montgomery. As they were on the highway behind one of the buses, the bus that they were following started to slow down, then came to a stop, and as my father's driver went around the bus slowly to see what caused the bus to stop off on the shoulder of the highway, a car was down in the woods and looked as if they had ran off the road. There were several cars off the side of the road shining their headlights down in the woods. It appeared to be a white woman behind the wheel and a black male. Since there was plenty of help there already, they continued to make their way back to Selma. By the time my father got home, my mother told him about the news on television about Mrs. Liuzzo, a white civil right leader who came from up North to support the movement and that he was shot and killed and the young black boy that she was giving a ride back to Selma after the march was not injured. He played dead when they shot into the car. Such a sad ending of such a great day. My father was exhausted and longed for a hot bath and a nice warm meal, and off to bed he went. On March 30, 1965, the Freedom Baby whom my father called by was born and was named Kathryn. I was the sixth child.

The Author as a baby, born March 30, 1965, named as the freedom baby, by the late Rev. Galloway

Chapter 6
Selma Visitors Off to Ipswich

A couple of months passed since the infamous march from Selma to Montgomery, and my father was already working on his next movement of making a difference. Rev. Virgil Wood, director of the SCLC, and James Reed, the youth coordinator at the Blue Hills Community Center, were working with Reverend Sherill on the program to make this trip happen to get some of the young freedom fighters up to Ipswich, Massachusetts. Reverend Sherill also discussed the trip with Andrew Young, executive secretary to Dr. King, when Dr. King and Andrew Young were in Boston that next month after the march. Heading up the Selma, an all-white suburb organizational work for the trip were Mrs. James Bevel, Rev. Fred Reese, a Selma high school teacher and president of the DCLV, and Rev. George Galloway Sr., my father and a Methodist minister and veteran freedom fighter and leader. Reverend Sherill explained to the organizers that the trip would offer the opportunity for a positive program of exchange of understanding between the heart of a metropolitan area, an all-white suburb, and a Southern city with its particular problems. He also stated that this trip for the thirty-six Selma black students could be educational and influential and to focus on Northern segregation, which was equally devastating. My father thought this place needed the help, and he wanted to make a difference and a change knowing that segregation in the North where job opportunity, social mobility, and housing were often denied to the blacks and the organization along with Reverend Sherill's thoughts of aiming at Ipswich and towns like it where the major potential for solving the problems or at least trying to make a change. My father knew that Boston was among the most segregated. Beginning in the 1960s, civil rights activists and the white liberal politicians had moved to integrate the city school imbalance, and in 1965, the state legislature passed the Massachusetts Radial Imbalance Act to do just that, and from the way Reverend Sherill was talking to him during their walk to Montgomery, he knew that the blacks in the Boston area were suffering and fighting the same cause that Selma was fighting.

The preparation for putting the trip together started out with Rev. Gilbert Caldwell, pastor of Union Methodist Church. South End Boston gave more than $7,000 to aid the newborn freedom fighter of Selma, Alabama. The proceeds of the recent rally will be presented to Rev. F. D. Reese, head of the Dallas Counter Voter League. These funds would be used to finance the continuing battle to register Negro voters, because at this moment, my father and only three hundreds have been registered to date out of fifteen thousand who are of voting age in the county. These Boston delegation group of rabbis was the most illustrious group of any section in the nation, and they were dedicated to helping push forward this movement. The bus trip was paid for by donations. The youth group of Ascension Memorial Church and the Episcopal Young churchmen voted that same week that the donation of $100 would be given for the trip. My father and the other organizers agreed that the estimated amount that need to be raised was $3,400 to pay for the trip. The bus alone costs nearly $2,000, and it will take approximately $114 a day to feed the busload. The bus vacation would be two weeks long, during which, the Southerners would spend time in Washington, DC; New York; Roxbury; Boston; and Ipswich, Massachusetts. There would be thirty-six students from Selma who have participated in recent civil rights activity and the Montgomery march that would be selected to go on this trip. My father wished George could have made this trip, but he wasn't old enough, but taking the students who knew what fighting for your rights is all about gave him honor and an opportunity. The process got underway, and application were given out to the students, and my father alone with Rev. Reese and Ms. Lilly and Mrs. Bevel picked the thirty-six students. The criteria they were looking for in the students were good grades, active involvement in the civil rights movement, and determination. They also were look-ing for students who wanted to go on this trip to learn and also help other rural towns get the blacks registered to vote. It did not take long to get plenty of applications back. In fact, they had more applications than they had available seats on the bus. However, they knew it was only thirty-six who could be selected, so they chose the students. My father said to the other leaders after completing the selection of students that "These young people that we selected to go have shown the country a determined approach to freedom," and he thought it would be a good for both the Northern communities and the Selma youngsters to visit with one another.

Rev. Galloway, taking civil rights students to Ipswich
Massachusetts to register black citizens to vote.

Chapter 7
The Ipswich Trip

The day finally arrived, and my father had everything ready. The travel itinerary was set, and my father and the organizer pulled the community together and sponsored a well-deserving trip. June 15, 1965, was a clear beautiful morning. The family was up for breakfast. as they sat at the table, my father prayed over the family, and then he told George to make sure he take good care of the ladies while he was gone. He kissed everyone goodbye and proceeded out the door. He stood on the porch that had an aluminum glider on it and a magnolia tree in full bloom in the front yard. He looked at the beautiful clear sky with the sun rising barely over the trees and said, "God, cover my family, and cover the entire group as we travel on the highway to and from our destination." He got in the car and looked at the front door. My mother waved goodbye, and he drove off heading to Brown Chapel. Upon arriving at the church, the chartered bus parked in front of the church, and parents were getting their kids on the bus. Mrs. Bevel and other organizers were assisting everyone in placing them on the bus. My father talked over the travel details, and he made a roll call of the thirty-six students on the bus. One of the young students by the name of Charles Peterson asked how long it would be before the bus was going to leave. My father answered, "In about ten minutes." The bus driver came onto the bus with my father, preparing to leave, and one of the students yelled out that a lady was walking fast toward the bus, waving her hands. The bus driver opened the door. It was Charles's mother telling my dad that she needed to give money to her son and that she was afraid the bus had already taken off. Charles got out his seat and came to the front of the bus, where my dad was and hugged his mom and took the money happy as he could be. He returned to his seat, smiling with joy. The bus slowly pulled away, and the parents were waving goodbye. Off they headed to Highway 80. My father was sitting in the front seat in the far right of the bus driver; and the other chaperone, Ms. Lilly, who was also my father's aide at his church, was sitting directly behind the bus driver. As they were on riding on Highway 80, my father had thoughts of four months ago. "This is where it all started with the walk from Selma to Montgomery," and now he is going to make a difference in Boston, a place where among the most segregated. Boston had its history of not wanting to integrate. There was even talk of forming a single district uniting white suburban and black urban schools, but all these plans met with resistance, particularly from the residents of Irish-American working class enclave of South Boston leading the judge to issue a court order.

There was work yet to be done not only in Selma but across the entire United States. The 824 miles to their first stop to Washington, DC, was a nice ride. They sang freedom songs, and the students played games among themselves, and just as they crossed over into the North Carolina State, they stopped and ate. My father had thoughts of when he went to college at A&T State University in Greensboro, NC, and how he used to travel the same highway to go back and forth to Danville, VA, to visit his grandmother and help her out at her merchant store on school breaks. They crossed over the Fourteenth Street Bridge around seven o'clock that evening, and the students got so excited seeing the lights shining on the National Monument standing in the middle of the National Mall and the Lincoln Memorial with lights shining directly on Abraham Lincoln. The students were so amazed at all the lights and traffic and skyscrapers. As they made their way to the hotel, the small restaurant where the kids ate dinner at was integrated, and blacks and whites were eating together something the students had never seen before because in Selma you could not walk on the same side of the streets as whites. After dinner, they were all tired from the trip, and they were assigned rooms and got some much-needed rest after the long ride. The next morning, they hit the ground running touring the

National Monument, the Lincoln Memorial and other museums in the city. That afternoon, they went to the White House for a tour of the White House and had an early dinner in the State Dining Room, which is the larger of two dining rooms on the state floor of the executive residence of the White House. This dining room had beautiful round tables set up for dinner with silverware correctly placed beside the beautiful white china dishes. The paneling was bone-white, and the silver-plated chandelier and wall sconce were matching serving tables. The mantle was of white marble to match the color scheme, and the long yellow goldish drapes were beautifully matched to the linen tablecloths that covered the tables. There were beautiful flower arrangements at every table with tulip-shaped crystal vases. The students and my father were much honored to be in the midst of such beauty and elegance and to see history and knowing that our black people built such a beautiful place. After the early dinner that ended around two o'clock, they traveled to Ipswich, Massachusetts, it was about an eight-hour ride. They arrived in Ipswich late Friday night tired but happy. A busload of thirty-six boys and girls and my father and Ms. Lilly were greeted by Rev. F. Goldwaite Sherill, rector of the Ascension Memorial Church.

They were given a roaring greeting as they got off the bus. Just as one of the female students got off the bus and stood beside a little white girl, the white girl grabbed the Selma student's hand and rubbed it and asked her, "Does it come off?" The student was confused and asked, "Does what come off?" The little white girl said, "This color." The student asked the little white girl if she had ever seen black people before, and the white girl told her no. The student told the little girl that even though she was darker in skin than her, they were still all the same in God's eye. The greeting was held at Boone Memorial Hall by some 150 weekend hosts and youth groups from Ipswich and Boston. Too exhausted to eat, the youngsters were taken to homes that they were assigned to after a short session of singing and greetings offered by Reverend Sherill and two Ipswich selectmen, Chairman John Pechilis and John Logan. Tired from the trip, my father had the meeting with the other organizers and went over the schedule for the week, and he then called it a night, in closing thanking God for a safe trip. On Saturday, June 19, morning following breakfast with hosts, the group gathered at Crane's Beach for a day of picnics and games. The Negro and white boys and girls swam together in the icy water at Cranes Beach, and for the first time, the Selma youngsters tasted steamed clams and crawfish. Edward Rauscher, police officer of Ipswich who with his wife and three children were hosts to Selma youngsters. Mrs. Rauscher said her daughter had never met Negros, and her oldest daughter, Deborah, could not understand why their Selma guest had been to jail, but when the Selma youth explained to her, she then understood more about the civil rights movement. The cold Atlantic wasn't inviting, but the visitors and hosts made the best of it. My father sat on the sand looking at the kids throwing football together and sitting around talking to one another; and he thought, "We made history again because there had never been any Negro to step foot on the Northern Shore Beaches with blacks and white swimming together." Theophilis Bailey, age fifteen, of Selma walked over to my father and said to him, "It took me until now to figure it out, but now I've got to the root of it. No Negros live here at all!" Here's the place that really needed the freedom movements. Because the Roxbury children had arrived ahead of the Selma children and in time to greet them, this young boy had not known right away that in terms of housing, job opportunities, and community acceptance. Northern segregation, although different in form, was deeply corruptive of the communities involved as is the Southern variety, but now the shadow of doubt had fallen, and as it fell upon him, it fell upon the sympathetic residents of Ipswich as well. How deeply concerned, "Are we with people after all? How committed are we to the ideals of our fathers, despite the slogan which describe us as the birthplace of independence?" My father quietly sat looking at this beautiful body of water that God created and began thinking that all this beauty and its not to be even shared for all eyes to see. It saddened one's heart to watch the Selma negro youth connect with the white youth, and they never encountered having a conversation with other races. Some whites had never seen a black person in their life, and the separation and hate are something that should never be taught in this world that God created. God is love.

The sight of trees and water was alien experience for many of the Selma students and know very little of the world outside of Selma. That's why my father stressed the significance of the contact between races which this weekend will produced. For many of the whites from Ipswich and the blacks from Selma and Roxbury had never before spent more than a few minutes talking to a member of the other race until now. My father was proud of what he was bringing together. He not only placed the Selma students in an environment that they would not have seen without this trip, but he arranged with locals around the town for nine of his Selma students to take their first plane ride in a private plane from Plum Island and circled the Northern shore. Another group mounted horses for the first time when Mr. and Mrs. Downey took a group to a Manchester stable. Others toured the Whipple House and Heard House, which were admission-free for the visitors. As the second day continued in Ipswich, many had changed their opinions of the project during the weekend and were frank to admit how pleasantly surprised they were. Those closest to the project were the happiest, obviously. Some were merely relieved that there had been no incident. Although, it wasn't clear to my father just what sort of incident might have taken place or who could have provoked such an incident, but it had been a worry to many for no reason. Some were still hostile. Others shrug their shoulders and said, "So what does all this prove?" My father answered, "The real question lay, however, not in the looking back at what a happy time those involved had enjoyed at Crane's Beach, riding horseback or in an airplane, or singing freedom songs, or attending church or just sitting around in the backyard. The deeper question behind all the talk pro and con, from hostile, anxious, or hopeful, all had to do with where do we go from here?" Especially when there were barriers raised which made it difficult for Negroes to settle in suburban communities and not to mention the state housing laws in place to housing unavailable to the blacks, these topics made the difference to many who deserve the same opportunity as everyone else. After a long day at the beach, the ministers of Ipswich and the hosts set up a big gathering at Boone Hall. They had cooked enough food to feed an army, and the entertainment started off with my father playing the piano, with everybody singing songs. Rev. Wendall Verill, Bill Downey III, Sally Cummings, and the Freedom Choirs from the three Negro groups performed as well. Sunday morning, the youngster attended church services in various Ipswich churches.

My father also led singing at Ascension Memorial Church on Sunday and told his congregation after one restrained verse of a hymn he thought that the atmosphere in this building right now needed some uplifting, so before he started the second verse, he stopped playing the piano and said to the congregation, "Now, you all, let's remember that Jesus is living, not dead, and let's sing like that too. We'll try it again now." A series of panel discussions scheduled for Sunday afternoon was called off because the weather was too fine, and the kids went back to the beach, so my father basically spoke to the locals and thanked them for the great hospitality. On Monday morning, the group went to Glouchester High School; and my father and his aide, Ms. Lilly, picked two girls, Aurilla McDonald and Georgia Moore of Selma, to attend a visitor at GHS to get the experience of congregating with students at an all-white school. Meanwhile, my father and Ms. Lilly met with Rev. John Elder of Annisquam, Rev. Frank Porter, Mrs. Ellen Gabin of Rockport, and Margaret Sullivan, a high school student to discuss civil rights and integrating the school which this topic my father knew too well and told the story of how his children integrated the school in Selma explained how the process could work there at GHS. He explained how determined these young freedom fighters had the passion and heart of a lion, and he went on to tell them the story about one of the students that's on this trip with him, Diane Pettaway, age fifteen, a sophomore at RD Hudson High School in Selma, describing how she was arrested three times in the demonstrations and how she and two other students helped two California clergymen integrate a Selma restaurant. They just sat there peaceful and quiet until finally they were served. Students had the fight in them and knew the sacrifices they needed to make to see a change for their future. These were the student youths, fourteen to eighteen years old, who gave up part of their summer school break to make a difference. They had not only a passion but a dream of a better tomorrow. The fight and sacrifices had to be real and taken

75

serious if this was something that the people sitting here at this table were willing to endure. The meeting ended on a positive note, leaving the people in Glouchester with much-needed information to get things rolling. Tuesday, they traveled to Roxbury for the rest of the week. Roxbury was different than Ipswich, full of refuse and litter. Once settled in Roxbury, they went to a fried chicken supper provided for the teenagers at the New Hope Baptist Church in Roxbury, and my father discussed how they were going to start the voters' rally on Wednesday. The community Voter Registration Project was sponsored by seven Boston Civil rights group as a part of an effort to get an estimated 26,000 unregistered residents of North Roxbury and Dorchester to vote.

Byron Rushing, youth coordinator of the registration project, urged the youths and their Roxbury counterparts to work to overcome the apathy found in many Negro sections. My father set up the teenagers and explained to them that they would have to go door-to-door of the North Roxbury neighborhood asking each unregistered adult to register to vote. They told the adults when and where to vote. Each person was asked if he would be interested in being a block captain who would urge others to register and to hold small educational classes in their homes and inform them of any information to help them to register. My father thought to himself that it's such a difference between Selma and Roxbury. In Selma, people go down to city hall to register in big numbers, but up there, we had to the walk the streets trying to encourage them to register. After a long day of the voters' drive, they end the day by leading a freedom march down Blue Hill Avenue, singing freedom songs with a lot of the blacks from Roxbury, and joining in with them, a big difference than Ipswich, where there were only two blacks families living there. They spent two more days assisting with the voters' rally. They went into the city of Boston on the last day, Friday, to have a sightseeing and going to many of the black neighborhoods talking with many of the Boston residents. They loaded up the bus on Saturday heading to the World's Fair for a day in New York City. The youngsters were so excited this fair was the second World's Fair to be held at Flushing Meadows Park. This was the largest World's Fair ever to be held in the United States occupying nearly a square mile of land. When they drove up on the grounds at the fair, they saw a large twelve-story high stainless steel model of the earth called Unisphere with the orbit tracks of three satellites encircling the giant globe. There were water fountains, rides and many vendors as far as your eye could see. They spent the entire day there and then loaded on the bus traveling back to Selma, they discussed on this long bus ride the experience they encountered and the friends they met. My father spoke to the youths on the bus saying that this trip was a great meeting the youth of Ipswich were touched by your stories and that this trip was the most constructive and spiritual fellowship, and the most important result of the weekend was that the Selma Negroes had a chance to see that there was more to life in the United States than what they had seen. The civil rights movement had a heartbeat, and there was no stopping it, and going to Massachusetts showed the students that Selma was not alone and that all blacks were in this fight together and they must make a stand and fight for our rights. He felt awesome, *wonderful*. He felt like young people hadn't abandoned the cause. They appreciated what they all did to try and clear the way for them. Seeing black and white students being photographed together in Selma was unheard of, and with prayers and determination, he hoped to see it come to pass.

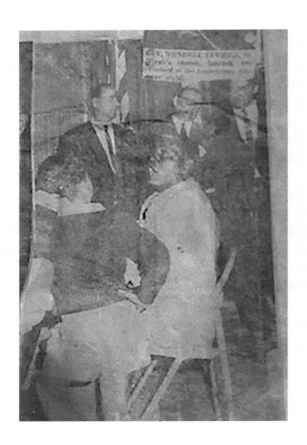

Rev. Galloway playing the piano during the meet
and greet in Ipswich Massachusetts.

REV. MARTIN McCABE, Rowley, talks with Rev. George Galloway, leader of the Selma visitors.

HYMN SINGING Friday was led by Selma's Rev. Galloway — a job he also holds at the famous Brown's chapel in Selma. Ipswich Selectmen John Pechilis, John Conley and John Logan back him up. Galloway also led singing at Ascension Memorial church Sunday and told his congregation after one restrained verse of a hymn, "Now, you all, let's remember that Jesus is living, not dead and let's sing like that too. We'll try it again now."

Rev Galloway meeting, with Rev. Martin McCabe, during the Ipswich Massachusetts trip.

The civil rights students from Selma, Alabama, which
Rev Galloway lead to Ipswich Massachusetts, joined
other host families children at the beach.

Rev. Galloway group of civil rights students, enjoy a day
at the beach during the Ipswich Massachusetts trip.

On the way to class at GHS

Two of the civil rights student, attend class at
Gloucester High School, as part of Rev. Galloway
meeting request, with the school board.

Chapter 8
History Doors to Open

They arrived back into Selma really early before day on Sunday morning. My father parked the Oldsmobile in front of the house and turned off the engine. The porch light was on, yellow and flickering with night bugs. He sat there for a minute and leaned over the steering wheel. He spoke to God and thanked him for his covering and bringing light to those people eyes in the cities that they visited. He then got out of the car, tired from the long trip, and entered the house. Everyone was in bed sound asleep. He walked thru the house and looked in on the children and went quietly to bed. The next morning, he sat at the dining room table and told my mother and older kids about the trip. He then gave my mother two beautiful ceramic ashtrays with Boston City engraved in them. He was excited to get back to his congregation not even feeling like he only had a couple hours of sleep. His juices were flowing, wanting to tell everyone about the trip and what the experience they all encountered. He spoke to his congregation, telling them not to give up, to keep fighting, and to never give in or give up. He added, "Grab all the resources that are available for you, and get yourselves ready to compete." He then turned to the young folks to tell them to take their education seriously. "I know that segregation isn't dead. Just look at schools and neighborhoods and workplaces, and you can see that it's still all over America. And yes, we are still at the very beginning economically. The civil rights movement will clear the way legally, so we can progress opening the doors for the younger generation. If we don't learn that it is our mothers, uncle, classmates, our neighbors, and many others who made and sustained the civil rights movement, then we won't know we can do it again for another cause, and then the other side wins even before we ever begin the fight." My father continued to speak to his congregation saying that "That trip has given me encouragement for the work before us." He then smiled at the crowd and smiled at my family and walked over to the piano and started playing his favorite song "God Is Not Dead" and told the congregation to "Join in, and let's give God some praise."

The Family of Music

Kathryn, the Freedom Baby, in her own words

This book contains a very personal and, I hope, moving story. On a warm summer night in 2015, after the fiftieth anniversary of the Selma to Montgomery march, I began writing what you will find in the pages of this memoir, memories and the life told from my father's words of his life of accomplishments. One of the most basic instincts we humans have is to process and give meaning to all of our experiences, both good and bad, and seek to more enrich for it. This is a book about the emotional landmarks, the struggles and determination to fight, to cross mountains and valleys of darkness with much hate and bigotry, the desert of despair, and the tidal waves of fate. As I was writing my father story, I started to wonder, though it felt like quite an indulgence, if people could perhaps be moved or inspired by my story, to take a stand and fight. I was too young to realize or know about the struggle of my people. I was born on March 30, 1965, in Selma, Alabama, the sixth child born to a family of music and many talents. My oldest sister was a pianist, and my oldest brother was a guitarist. We all were raised singing together as a group and love the Lord. However, growing up in Selma as a little girl, the memories are instilled, from remembering my godmother, Sister Strugg, to going to my father church singing and shouting praises for God. The unequal world of segregation between a black person and a white made it impossible to know whether what flowed between two people was honest feelings or pity or pragmatism. But what I am sure about is this: through the flows of life, through the challenges, the opportunities, the change perspectives, welcome exposure to the new. I will resist the urge to go back to what the whites are so familiar with:

the power of exposure to the fight that my father believed in, and it made not only myself but my siblings as well to not go back to the old situation. I was raised in a household who taught us to focus on what lies ahead and then believe in God's power to take me there. My father, mother, and many of the freedom leaders' priorities were set toward destiny. They were aware of where they were and where they were trying to go. And I believe if you are aware, you are prepared to seize opportunities as they arise. "Narrow is the way to life and few find it" (Matthew 7:13–14). I have wished, for many years, that I had been old enough and thoughtful enough to ask more questions when he was still on this earth. Unfortunately with his passing, I've spent years imagining his entire story needing to be told. And this is why I wrote this book.

The work never stops, the freedom baby Marching during an event in Birmingham Alabama.

The freedom baby attending the jubilee in Selma Alabama, as of today, the protesters are still Marching.

Photo at Selma Jubilee celebrating my father's legacy

The family that March together stays together, and The late civil rights leader, Rev. Galloway, watches his legacy.

Galloway's third generation celebrates their grandfathers legacy at jubilee in Selma

Rev. Galloway determined his children would get a quality education. Two kids, first to integrate Byrd elementary school.

About the Author

The Author the freedom baby, Kathryn Galloway-James

Kathryn Galloway James, a native of Selma, Alabama, was born in Selma and grew up in Andalusia, Alabama. I received a dental hygiene technology associate degree at Nova Community College in Annandale, VA, in 1991. I spend a lot of my time working with the Lake County Supervisor of Election, working at over one hundred precincts to assist voters in the voting process and getting people registered to vote. I currently reside in Eustis, Florida, with my husband.

Lightning Source UK Ltd.
Milton Keynes UK
UKHW042208020419
340367UK00001B/47/P